JAGGED EDGE
OF THE SKY
A NOVEL

PAULA MARIE COOMER

FAWKES PRESS

Cover Design by Greg Simanson
Edited by Nancy Casey

PRINT ISBN 978-1-945419-02-7

EPUB ISBN 978-1-945419-03-4

Library of Congress Control Number: 2016901688

AUTHOR'S NOTE

I wrote this novel to be accurate for its time both during the 1950s in Western Australia and later in the century in the US. Because of this I have used words that we might consider inappropriate today with regards to certain groups of people. It was not my wish to offend, therefore I offer my apology to anyone who might find my choices wrong or abrasive.

Also, some readers might be confused by the handling of time in *Jagged Edge of the Sky*. To paraphrase 19th century philosopher Georg Hegel, time is a construct, relative only as it relates to change. *Jagged Edge of the Sky* attempts to reveal a story by noting changes in characters' lives apart from clocks and calendars. Because of this, the book moves non-sequentially and leaves a number of unanswered questions, the resolution of which are left to the reader's imagination. In fact, it would appear that one character does not age at all.

For Daddy

For history is a pontoon bridge. Every man walks and works at its building end and has come as far as he has over the pontoons laid by others he may never have heard of.

—Wallace Stegner in *Wolf Willow*

PART I

MORGAN BOSWICK

CROUCHED AND HANGING by the arms from a pair of ancient shipping barrels, Morgan pushes her baby out onto the straw-stuffed bed she prepared ahead of time, cuts the cord with a cane knife, then hovers over the pail and cramps hard against the placenta. The smell of copper and the sound of the baby's bawling overtakes everything else. She examines the boy, sees no reason for concern, swaddles him with a piece of an old bedsheet, and holds him close to her chest for a few moments. To the best she can figure, the spot where the south and west walls of the loft meet is the safest for the moment, so that's where she secures the baby. No fear of the dark, she carries the mess down the ladder, dumps it a few dozen meters into the bush for the goannas, and what few dingoes remain about. Beyond the perimeter of her small plot of ground, the bush feels suspended. Nothing good or bad or indifferent about. Just the night air hanging, waiting.

She's trying to get the wriggly thing to latch its gosling-cheep of a mouth onto her nipple when Jimmy D. drives up. He pounds the century-old door a loud once then bursts in massaging his fist and spouting profanities, scanning the scene. He asks whether the boy belongs to him or that bastard dark-haired American bloke—Jimmy D. himself as dark as his mother.

Morgan looks at him. Which one do you think?

Think he's bloody well mine, Jimmy D. says. Best be, or I'll carve the lot, too right.

Which is the story she decides to tell.

Morgan names him Robby. After her father, Robert, who, once he's into his pints, his mates call Robert the Bruce. A stain marks the base of the infant's skull. A stork bite—almost the exact same shade of pink as the once-red handkerchief she uses to wipe blood and birth from the boy's body and face.

PART II

CHERISE MARIE TUOR

ONE BABY IN THE PRAM and a second in her belly.
A girl this time, she figured—a girl in the quiet corners of her
mind she was already calling Annalesa—because the position-
ing of the fetus was distinct from the way it was with Piotr,
her first. Also because the old midwife, Adelle, had come with
Dreamtime stories to tell her so. A girl who will bear responsibility, Adelle said.

September still clung to the calendar, here in the southwest
the wet still a bit distant. October was days away, spring definitely coming on. Here she was, full as a goog again. Cherise
rolled the pram along the lane to the main house. To carry and
birth a child in the heat of a southern hemisphere summer was
a mother's last wish, she knew as fact. Piotr had come into the
world nine months prior, smack on Christmas Day, unexpect-
ed as Jesus. He was due the middle of January, when it would
have been hotter still and which made the early birth a grateful
point.

Even so, the heat left a mark on her not yet resolved.

All it took was thinking about Piotr to stir him. He'd wig-
gled loose a foot, and even though he was wrapped in a coverlet from neck to ankles, she still worried he'd catch the grippe.
Stocking your head and feet and you'll not fall ill, her father had
always said. Imagine, a baby as young as Piotr hating socks on
his feet. Trying to get that one in his leather shoes was harder
than snubbing a bushfire. If the mother hens in Denton could
be believed, he'd never learn to walk. Cherise thought a tap to
the withers with a length of cane would do him good, but the
boy's dad, her husband Edmonds, bid her not to raise a hand.
Her own father had smarted her backsides often enough, but
Edmonds wouldn't hear of it.

The boy was born without socks and shoes, Edmonds said,

going out of the house that morning. Might be he's quicker than the mob of us.

Cherise leaned over the pram, touched her nose to the foot and let the soft smell pass to her heart. She ran her finger along the creased print of the sole, crinkled as a miswritten check, tucked the foot back under the coverlet, then straightened, leveraging her palms against the small of her back. The noon sun struck her face, and she smiled, aware of her lips, her teeth. Cherise breathed deeply as she had of Piotr's foot, willing spring to enter and excite the unborn possible-girl into an early appearance as well. She smoothed her own damp brow. Such exertion it had become, bending and straightening. Ah. Sun. You befriend me, she said.

Then back onto the dust lane of the caravan park. If her mother were still about, bless her, she'd think it rotten, a daughter of hers married to the overseer of such a place. But for Edmonds, caravans were the future slung all the way from America and from far back in Australia's history, and therefore, a service to his countrymen.

Chaps was pulling wood wagons full of their life necessities for coming up on a century, Cherise, he'd said in one of their early conversations about the subject. It's caught on in America. This is America's new Conestoga, you mind me. In twenty years, every bloke will own one. Same goes for Australia, and the rest of the world, too, luv, and we've got the first and the best right here at the edge of Jelico. Pull toilets and a petrol cooktop! And think of the people! All the types to meet, Cherise. And look. Only ones can afford them are blokes with cash. We won't be slaves to wages ever again, Cherise. Think of all the babes. All the ones yet to be born to us, luv. Don't you want for them?

Edmonds, long as a staff, fair-eyed and thin-browed, was forever looking to spark something new — first the land outside Jelico, and then the turn at blacksmithing. Blacksmithing! He reasoned there to be plenty of wild brumbies yet to be caught and broke. Still shoes to be fired and hammered. If not, then fancy ironwork for the tradesmen's houses going up in the wake of the war. The entire district had laughed, calling him Noah. A Swiss councilor's son telling himself a story, thinking to make it occur in the real world.

But there are barely tracks and most only swished out with a broom, Cherise had said. Who is going to tow a caravan about the bush? Most men around here are barely capable of keeping their utes in rubber and petrol, and sure aren't apt to be pilfering pound notes from their wives' sugar bowls to buy a caravan. This isn't America, Edmonds. If you wanted America, why in bloody hell didn't we just go to America? Certainly would have been cheaper.

Ah, Cherise. Let a man dream, will you? Let a man dream, he had said. So they leveled places and planted gorse and hollyhocks and clematis on trellises and blue everlastings and strung electrical wire to the petrol generator. Edmonds forged his curlicues and iron railings for little patios. No one came and no one came until he finally dawned his idea to buy a pair of caravans and lend them out parked, like a road station. The Reserve Bank now held the note against both the caravans and the big house they were living in—itself rescued and rebuilt from station salvage, but in the genius way of Edmonds. They journeyed to Perth putting notices and bought advertisements in the print news from *The Denton Record* to Melbourne's *Sentinel*, for all the good any of it would do, as Cherise reminded Edmonds every time a bill showed up in the post.

I'll buy me a bloody road sign in Sydney, I will, Edmonds had said. But before the week was out, Barry Gibson and Nathan Cleary had arrived, assigned to help carve the Jelico end of the very track Edmonds hoped would change his fortune and who would eventually meet a larger crew working their way from Perth.

***

Had Cherise been less annoyed with her life in general and with Edmonds' endless stream of ideas, which ranged from the park's water tanks to the new widow's deck with its silly iron stairs, hand-forged in his shop, spiraling to the porch below, she might have sidestepped the night in 1951, not six months after her second child and only daughter Annalesa was born, when Rich Hand first slid her dress to her hips and thrust himself into her, donating the milk-pale secretions that mixed with parts of her to become her third baby—the boy Martin. She might have sidestepped the secret life it caused her to create for herself. Might have sidestepped having to watch the belly of Jeanne McMurtrey, which swelled over the weeks at the same rate as hers, as Jeanne was first an emotional wreck and then so beset with morning sickness that the clan stayed on much longer than was originally planned. Bad enough the mess occurred. Even worse that they refused to leave, no matter how much cash they were pouring in, as Edmonds had upped their space rent to double the agreed-upon rate. Cherise at night lay awake staring at the whitewashed ceiling. The wood planks swelled and blanched with the heat, the drought, the wet, enticing the flies to lay black-speck eggs in the joints between them. On her back next to Edmonds, while the American woman Jeanne McMurtrey lay on the other side of the Outbound beside her husband Russell, Cherise imagined ripping the boards loose and making good use of the nozzle end of a squirt can full of fly-ending poison.

Except that Rich Hand *had* come at her, his hands, muscled between the web of thumb and forefinger that she had so longed to kiss, running somewhat forcefully up the slide of her thigh into the wetness that had been there since the moment he arrived. Fingers thrusting into her, pumping like a generator piston, at the rate of her own pulse, until she could do nothing save put her own force into it, ram against his ramming, the power exiting as an exclamation from her throat and through the cavern of her lower body, both of them looking at the right moment to see the juices stretched in tendrils when he pulled out fingers and replaced them with the male part of himself, the fullness nearly more than she could stand. She felt herself, red and engorged and silently begging for him. Annalesa's milk, which seeped from her breasts through to her dress, dripped down her sides. The sensation setting her hips battering more frantically, until at last the final white explosion forced a piece of Rich Hand toward the tiny world of her egg.

The minute beginnings of a boy fused.

Martin. Two syllables, as if on a blackboard, wrote themselves in dusty chalk on Cherise's forebrain. She almost whispered them but caught herself, lest Rich think she was calling to another man.

Miss. Please. Uh, I don't know, Miss. I've been fighting myself. Yesterday I couldn't have said for certain I was bound to do that. But today. I don't know. I thought about it, but I couldn't have said for certain, Rich said, leaning against her, their mingling further dampening their clothing, congealing, the smell like rising bread.

Straightening herself and her dress with one hand, she pushed Rich away with the other. Leave, she said. You must go. You know it. Edmonds will figure it out, and he will lay you open. Please take me. What you don't know is I want to go, too. I want to leave.

Leave behind your Annalesa? Still a suckling? You've a boy in the pram, too, I reckon? Rich said. Walk off from your entire family for a stranger of a bloke and a new mess?

Yes, she said, God help me. Annalesa is still a suckling. Who you are is mystery for now, but not for long, if we work at it.

Well, sure I can take you out of it, Rich said, but the law and my money says the husband will set sail to claim ownership.

They were in the sleeper, full of grog, the sheets dampened. Rich had his lips on her ear. A pearl of an ear, Edmonds had always called it. We'll have us a party, Rich was saying. We both know we're hooked together just for the moment. I say, so be it, but let's have us some fun and build a memory big as the Kimberley.

Cherise giggled to hide the catch in her throat. All right, she said. Meanwhile the track rolled between Denton and Gillagong, the wide nothing growing broader and broader, the two rising from their private activity now and again to smoke cigarettes, share tinnies of beer, nibble the shortbreads and nuts Rich had purchased and packed along, just because Cherise asked for them. She learned early in her marriage that asking for gifts from Edmonds, no matter how small, did not translate to delivery. She remembered once staring at a candy shop in Perth, saying how she'd like a truffle and Edmonds reminding her of its effect on her waist and his wallet. Rich was the opposite. I'd love you wide as a house if I was the one made you that way, he said when she asked for the treats and explained that history.

Somewhere late in the night, the train throbbing across the bush, Cherise awakened not to the milk-full sensation arisen in her breasts, although she realized the sheets were damp with their leakage, but of Rich climbing onto her. He did not make a sound, nor did she, and for truth, she did not think him fully awake, because not once did he open his eyes, rather hung over her with his handsome, dark face lunging straight ahead, black hair glinted here and there with whatever light was filtering in, his chest a road map of fine beads of sweat, his nipples brooding as the night itself, pulsing closer, retreating, coming back toward her again. Cherise watched, taking in every angle, conscious of the tight cord inside herself, cinching and releasing. She stifled her gasps, clamping involuntarily against Rich's length of engorged blood and muscle.

Now the surge between her legs, against her will, the voltage jarring her hips and thighs, her oceans releasing, the stream leaking between the hillocks of her bum. Rich kept pumping, not losing rhythm, as the train wailed, sending its plume toward the night. He was indeed asleep. How long he kept at it, she didn't know, for she dozed herself, only awakening when he rolled back to his side of the berth.

* * *

Gillagong the next morning was dusty, visibility poor because of a slow whirlwind tripping along the narrow streets and passageways. With it, bits of trash and twigs, and the occasional whiff of animal from the taxidermist. Cherise and Rich got off the train, her two satchels and his knapsack loaded with what few possessions they'd deemed necessary for the immediate future. Rich had dispensed with shirt and trousers, switched instead to the expected Outback attire: shorts, boots, and socks. Cherise wore a cotton dress and slip, the dress a plain, window-pane aqua, the slip loathsome in the heat but necessary to cover the cotton-stuffed brassiere staying her breasts' seepage. Even though she had pumped herself, she yet produced enough to satiate a six-month-old. Poor Little Annalesa. Edmonds would have to feed her canned milk and Karo. And Piotr. Little bumbler. What a sad case of a mom she was being.

They found a room above the pub, walked through its Saturday regulars and hanging tobacco smoke amidst loud whispers and a low whistle. Cherise felt the hair on her arms, shivered despite the swelter, felt the pulse behind her belly. She longed momentarily to be back safe with Edmonds, but she had cast her lot, and so, no going back. The barman led them up a stairway; the walls of it coated in mud-wash stained a vibrant but stony rust, like iron hinges hit by rain. Cherise swallowed against a surge of nausea. A sudden note of fear took hold. As was the case with Jeanne McMurtrey, both her pregnancies had made her instantaneously ill.

The pub owner was a huge bowl of a man, great of height

and limb, bent forward at the middle as if a toppled sack of grain. A murder of rooks and a series of yellow lightning bolts tattooed to his upper arms, the rounds of his back muscle boasting from a sleeveless vest. Such fair skin. As if he stayed inside most of the time. This contrast was heightened by the vest's black leather, lasted in front with a mismatched strip of bootlace, almost the same brown as his head of hair. The same brown as the seepage from the wad of tobacco bulging from his left cheek. The man leaned to divest himself of a stream of spittle aimed with an accuracy Cherise could have fairly well predicted at the lard tin positioned outside the guestroom door, then opened their room with a fob of keys, each silver, each long and with the ancient squared cleat meant to match a specific set of tumblers. Cherise loved the secrets of locks. She had a hidden collection of what she referred to within herself as dinosaur keys. She was fond of rummaging through bins at Denton's open market, bargaining with junk traders over their value—one shilling or two, halfpence. Once she laid down a full pound note for a pair of gold ornate keys said to have belonged to the Queen's own pantry, carried to Australia by a chap arrested for thievery. She doubted the truth of it but kept a note stuck to them in hopes, in the event of her death, her family could have faith she at least intended to leave them something of value.

The furnishings were oddly feminine in an otherwise rough-hewn environment. White chenille on the bed and lace for curtains. The window, closed against the dust, was so filmy as to be barely translucent, and a drift of pink dust lined the sill. Rich handed the pub owner three pounds. Thanked him and closed the door. Our humble abode, Rich said, his dark handsomeness spread out like a mural, patting the mattress. Climb aboard.

Cherise thought she was tired of sex, but gave of herself to please Rich. The work of their bodies compounded the heat, and she asked if he thought he might find her a bit of ice. Ice?

he said, louder and with more disdain than Cherise thought he ought to. Ice? A pair of warm pints and cold chips is more like it out here, ain't it, luv?

At which point she walked across the room to the wood commode with its flower-painted porcelain pitcher and bowl and gauzy towel across the rack, and upset her morning meal.

***

Bollocks. I'd sooner be dead as night as see that clan again. To Jelico? Back here? After nigh onto thirteen years? Edmonds said when Cherise showed him the letter. His hands were covered in plant pitch. He'd been pulling stragglers in shucks from a neglected garden patch. Cherise had begged him to clear it and to install a spout to divert their gray water and fashion a wooden irrigation canal running from the house, as she fancied a rose garden. Snow Whites and tea roses. American Beauties, Blue Glory, Savannahs. She'd fingered the pages of catalogs for months, telling herself that in a fair world, a woman always could depend on a rose garden to brighten whatever gloom she could not otherwise shake.

The letter refolded and back in its packet, Cherise took her husband's chin in hand, forcing his eyes to meet hers, an act as surprising as it was both strange and out of order. Not since that afternoon in Gillagong had she stood face to face with Edmonds. They talked from across the room or over their shoulders while engaged in activity.

To Perth for a night, then Denton. Day after tomorrow, more like. Or the next. They'll be here before midday they say, whatever day it ends up being. Fancy a cuppa while we get used the idea? she said to Edmonds, who turned to gaze at the far distance.

Perfect, Edmonds said. Give me cause to scrub off this soot while I think of someplace rather than here to put myself for the balance of the week.

First to the pump for water, then to the kitchen to fill the kettle and spoon tea-leaves into the pot. It seemed right to use her wedding porcelain, which was from France and hand-painted with blue cornflowers and kept closed tight in a pie safe in the far corner of the kitchen. The sheer white batiste covering the nine-pane over the sink translated the full-on sunlight to faint streaks, all of which was muted by the green canvas portico shading the west-facing veranda. The propane ring on the cooktop fired as she touched the lit match to it, the sulfur smell and hiss of fire passing vaguely through her consciousness until the flame level bid her to focus on it, so accustomed she was to this activity. The flame faded from orange-blue to white, and Cherise thought she might put her head to it, catch herself afire and have it be done. The sweeper brushes rattled, the sound blurred by its trip down the corridor. Martin cleaning his room again. The boy couldn't seem to clean it enough to satisfy himself. She ran her hands down the front of her belly, her mind barreling back to those few days with Rich Hand. Standing at the sink, she viewed the sum of her existence: the graveled pads with their caravans parked and trimmed with Edmonds' forged-iron decks and rails, the veggie garden, the clustered playground where Annalesa and Piotr took turns launching little Barney, the youngest—and her last kid, since she found out about a particular tincture she could purchase from Adelle to stop all that—in his favorite swing. Cherise pulled the biscuit tin off the shelf and counted five shortbreads, three for Edmonds, two for her. A spot of canned milk in the creamer, which Edmonds loved almost as much as the biscuits. A linen napkin, embroidered by Edmonds' mother many decades ago. The petals of a flower, white on white, had threads pulled loose in places.

She did not want it, the memory, but it grew until she gave in to it.

They were all in Gillagong. The McMurtreys a pace away, engaged in their own private but loud exchange. Edmonds shaking the leverage tool in her face. He was screaming an angry stream, spewing words she couldn't completely distinguish, blood vessels popping as if having lost their connection with the ribbed muscles of his neck and temples. Screaming, screaming, screaming, until she began her own barrage, willing him to hit her, to crack her skull wide open, which he did, not with the leveraging tool but with his open palm. Not so hard as all that, but hard enough to startle both of them, which Edmonds countered by taking his deep voice even louder, louder than she had ever heard a human voice, like the bellow of a kettle drum, until her eardrums were so full of blood they blocked it all off, and, momentarily deaf, she slumped to the ground.

Russell then stepped in, put a hand to Edmonds' shoulder and took the leverage tool from him. He reached for the hollow of Cherise's arm and helped her to stand, guided her to the Vanguard where she stood weeping into her palms. Eventually the four—Cherise, Russ, Jeanne, and Edmonds—had driven off, leaving Rich Hand bloody and kneeling on the street.

Cherise and Jeanne sat next to their respective husbands on the trip back. The McMurtreys in the rear seat. Edmonds driving. Not a word spoken. Cherise felt sure that Jeanne had an inkling same as she did: the dashing hired man had been common with them both.

The kitchen curtains moved with the exhale of her breath. She stared at the tray and the pretty cups. Tapped the strainer against one of them lightly. In her mind it was simple but urgent. Jeanne and Russell McMurtrey for reasons known only to the gods were returning after more than a decade to the Outbound. All right, but it would be she and not Edmonds who would not be there. Her entire existence in this place amounted to dead rot, as far as she was concerned, and she no longer wanted to claim one iota. All these years stuck sweltering away at the Outbound. She'd take a change of dress and changes of underclothes enough to get her across the continent, plus a wrap, and that was enough. That was all the memory she wanted.

Brief stairs led to the new add-on housing a loo with pumped water adjacent to her and Edmonds' shared bedroom. *See you around like a toilet seat.* Martin and his mates always said to each other at the end of a day of play. In the end, she tossed two extra shifts from the robe into a grip with a dozen pairs of underclothes and as many sets of anklets. The kettle began its tweet, then the full-on whistle. No one likely could hear her because of it, and no one could see her if she left under the clematis arbor by the back gate. Not a bloody one of them would miss her until suppertime. Edmonds would forget his tea. Martin's vacuuming would go on for an hour.

Then again, as the whistle on the teapot grew demanding, she feared Edmonds might come to tend it and interrupt her departure, so she stepped back into the kitchen to turn the flame dial to off, then to the rack by the kitchen door for her favorite hat—a little white-ribboned cloche she used primarily for trips to town. She placed it atop her head, smoothed her hair behind her ears, and was out the door. The bright sun bit at her, but the hat's brim covered enough of her face to shade her eyes and keep the burn off her nose. The hook latch on the picket gate lifted and re-latched without making a sound.

The park's lane looked for some reason longer than normal, but still welcoming. She had no sense that anything close to freedom lay beyond it, but that was not what she hoped for in any case. Freedom was not the chit on the table. Variety was. What was missing from her existence was variety. How certain she was about this action, this placement of feet. As sure as she had been about repainting the house, about accompanying Rich Hand. She put forward one foot, then the other, and before she knew it, the newly oiled dirt of the Drury Road was right in front of her. She hadn't a water bag, rationalizing that it was a Monday. Somebody headed to Jelico or Denton was apt to come along.

After perhaps an hour's walk, a clearly hard-run ute wad-
dled by and stopped. A young woman, hair pulled behind her
neck in a braid, wearing dungarees and a checkered shirt, sat
behind the wheel. Hop up, she called, ticking her head to the
passenger side. Water's in the canteen. Call me Jenny Kay. I'm
heading on the long road to Port Augusta. Will that help you?

A Yank. Cherise climbed into the dusty vehicle, her smile
involuntary, uncapped the canteen and allowed the water into
her mouth and throat. She drank long and deep, not realizing
how thirsty she actually was.

Sorry, Cherise said. Such a glutton.

I've got enough, the woman said, pointing to a pair of large
zinc jugs in back then reached to shake Cherise's hand. Where
do you need to get to? she asked, in distinct Yank fashion,
striking a box match against its striker, holding the lit end to a
manufactured cigarette.

Sydney. I'll get the train in Port Augusta, I reckon.

Well, you're fine to accompany me all the way if you like.
It'll take a few days, and I planned to sleep in back, but there's
room. You're not carrying much for someone going all the way
to Sydney. Good thing it's November. Death in the family?
Well, whether you go by train or stay with me, you won't make
the wake if it's anytime soon.

Cherise turned her head and stretched at the neck a bit to
avoid the rollover bar blocking her vision. No one was running to catch her, but part of her wished for it. Just something
to prove she was part of Edmonds' wish. In what seemed like
less than a minute, the questioning abandoned, Jenny Kay had
the machine up to speed, turning the Drury Road into a pink
boll of dust behind it.

For the second time in her life, Cherise found herself strug-
gling to put thoughts of her children out of mind, in particular
this time, her oldest son Piotr. The kid had been besieged by
night terrors his entire life, and they'd grown ten times worse
in the months prior to her leaving. Like he'd known what she

was going to do before she herself did. No brain to calculate what to do for him. Or about him. Her worries deep enough that she wrote Edmonds a letter mentioning Piotr's troubles. Jenny Kay promised to drop it by the Outbound on her way back to Denton for supplies, and before turning deeper into the bush toward the stopover called Gillagong, where she lived. Odd place for an American alone, Cherise thought, and her not much more than a girl, but what a help and benefit she turned out to be. Taught Cherise to smoke and drink shots of American bourbon, as a result of which Cherise told her about Rich Hand, about being one of two women living side by side for an occasion of weeks before the McMurtrey one departed back to her home in the US, both of them progressing in girth continents apart, debauched by the same man, sharing by telepathy the months of swelling and self-hatred. Wondering, on the day of Martin's birth, in between labor pains and the smell of sweat, and Adelle the midwife calling instructions to Edmonds, if Jeanne McMurtrey were giving birth, too. If the product of Jeanne's primal effort was the same as Cherise's, a boy with a thick whorl of near-black hair, dark-cream skin, the slope of Rich Hand's courting eyes. Just as she was wondering now whether the boy was, similar to Martin, turning out to be the sweet plum of everybody's heart.

Cherise and Jenny Kay sat in the ute for a number of minutes in the hot, open air at the train station at Port Augusta, south and east of Perth by several days' drive. They'd talked all four arms off over the course of three days, now in the end neither was speaking. Finally, Jenny Kay cleared her throat, saying, if it wasn't this it would be something else, Cherise. You did your job. You had him and got the rest this far. You'll get to Sydney. You'll take a break, and the weeks will tell what happens from there. Take time to catch up to yourself. Sounds like nobody's noticed how badly this crap has worn on people. I'm starting to learn why women look old before men. Most of what's hard falls to us. They just get drunk and go on.

I was brought up not to crave notice, Cherise said, after which they shook hands, hugged, and then parted.

Jenny Kay's initial letter arrived general post within days of Cherise's settling into a boarding situation. Piotr's troubles had escalated and earned him a lockup in the mental ward at Sisters of Hollywood Hospital in Perth. The note featured full mention of a conversation with Merl Chatcolet—the local law and the one who had to truss Piotr and transport him. Merl had been constable dating clear back to before Piotr was born. He'd seen a lot of hurt over a lot of dirt, Jenny Kay wrote, but packing a young man he watched grow up into a strap-coat troubled him. She went on to say that he had mulled his disharmony over pints at Jenny Kay's pub several nights in a row until he got over it.

After searching around a bit, Cherise finally decided to train as a nurse at Holy Cross Sanitarium in Sydney, for the steady work it would bring. She found herself feeling less angry with life and the world when she was working with her charges. Turned out to be good at chemistry and had an appreciation for the scientific theories behind the care she gave people. Getting her own flat came later, since the sisters at Holy Cross required trainees to live in quarters until the transition to graduate nurse, which allowed her ample time to save the bond for a flat. Once on her own, off-duty time was filled with nurturing flower starts and hemming white muslin squares to be used as napkins for the hospital's auxiliary to sell. Acquaintances drew themselves to her one by one. Of an evening, she drank a short glass of American bourbon, a habit she planned to keep, and smoked exactly three of the manufactured cigarettes Jenny Kay also had taught her to crave. It was the first inhalation at the end of the day she loved, plus the vague twitch that initially jangled then calmed her nerves. She thought of evenings that way—the golden time. Glass of golden bourbon. Golden tobacco. Golden glaze over the day, her life, and all of it. Cherise discovered after a while she did not pair with regret.

She thought guilt should follow a mom's abandonment of her kids, but it had not transpired that way. After Jenny Kay, she never again felt the urge to share her story. Every few weeks a patient with miscarriage or hysterectomy or stillbirth would be assigned to her ward. Secrets sometimes developed into talents, she had learned, and hers transformed into a gift for soothing the tears of women stunned by tragedy, who made comment on it, such that as time went on, the chief nurse regularly made them Cherise's charges. Those first years in Sydney were in truth the happiest of her life. A credit she owed to helping people in this way.

And to the golden time.

EDMONDS TUOR

THE QUESTION WAS whether Edmonds had it in him to kill Rich Hand. He'd give these city folks a taste of the bush. He sat in the passenger seat of his own plain-gray Vanguard with the windows cranked down, arm hanging out, fisting and unfisting his hand, the air catching his palm as if a ball in a mitt. The timing was hazy enough for him to doubt Jeanne and Russell McMurtrey's claims. Hand and Cherise were missing, true, as were both Cherise's satchels, but that only meant Hand might have gone off on his own for a bit of a walkabout, since he was of the type to take leave without sharing plans. Cherise could've loaned him the satchels and drove him to his departure place in the Clearys' auto. In the bush, people shared such things without question. Although he also had noted that at the time the Clearys themselves weren't at home. Still could mean the mob of them had nicked off to Jelico or Denton to market, or even further yet, headed into the bush to act like tourists in Gillagong—undependable and fickle as those road types could be—stopping for a spot of tea or a pint before the long return trip home. It was easy enough to see it as a possibility.

That Cherise hadn't left a note *was* peculiar, but Cherise had been peculiar all-around of late and prone to peculiarities by nature. For example, the jangle of keys in her jewelry drawer, now that was an odd lot, and the note: *The Queen's Pantry*, which Edmonds thought was a novel she meant to acquire through the post, as she sometimes did. Like his mom before, Cherise was always reading books. Plus, those sachets she trotted about, placing in niches around the house, herself regularly sniffing the air as if at something putrid. Edmonds never quite did pick up the scent she detected, although that didn't disallow its being, crippled at smelling things as his proboscis of a nose sometimes was.

The other offshoot, of course, was little Piotr, still a toddler and needing his mom, and Annalesa, who was only six months out of the womb. After living through the mother's milk experience when Piotr was born, Edmonds knew enough to know Cherise would be fevered if the baby did not suckle. In which case he was certain Cherise was only taking herself a day holiday in town with the Clearys. They'd be back quick enough.

But this American chap McMurtrey was insistent. His wife Jeanne was insistent. They argued loud when Edmonds said he believed Hand and Cherise had gone off on a friendly, casual day holiday with the Clearys and nothing more.

The louder they got the harder Edmonds argued it. All the way up to the point when the Clearys, in their flivver, came rattling up Drury Road.

Now see this? McMurtrey had said. *Here come the Clearys and no sight of the other two.* Insistent. As if the bloke wanted the bad outcome.

Edmonds still refused to believe it, until there it was, the Clearys, once they'd gotten out and dusted themselves, calmly reciting the fact that Rich Hand and the Missus Tuor had gone off. They hated to be part and pardon to it, they said, but Hand offered them fifty quid. Bonnie good money. Fifty quid! Bloody hell! Daft to pass up fifty quid. Bloody sorry, mate, but you know how hard a day we live in, Nate Cleary had said. Edmonds supposed a more inferior man would have knocked Nate through his teeth, but he had been in the same hardpan place as most of his tenants, the Clearys included. Never would he step in and part friends over fifty quid with a chap who'd been in on the start of this place, who had helped him lay peat and gravel, pound board and iron into porches and rails. Nate Cleary saw a chance to earn payment, did a job he was hired to do. Edmonds pulled off his lenses by the wire frames, cried outright, wiped his face with his handkerchief, then said, Saw her off safe and properly, then, did ya? Reckon I'm in debt to ya for that one.

What? Russell had said. You oughtta knock hell out of them.

An understanding between mates, Mr. McMurtrey. Nothing sadistic. Now let's be off. Annalesa will be needing her mum. And little Piotr cried himself to sleep. Good onya, mate. You be the driver. It's my flivver, but my eyes are used to the bush. I'd be a better lookout. Might be I'm more likely to spot a mob of roos before they mow us down than you would.

Aussies, Russell McMurtrey said, moving behind the wheel. The Vanguard ratcheted, caught, and fired its four cylinders, sounding slightly breathless until it broke into momentum.

Edmonds didn't respond. Twenty minutes down Drury Road he finally said, My father was from Switzerland. A banker and a counselor. Came here to save my mother suffering the Great War. Him wealthy and she a beaut. I grew up in Melbourne and studied at uni. And that's all there is to the story. Except for Cherise.

He felt on the verge of cracking. Dread pulled at his groin. His mother and father nearly forgotten. The easy days of Melbourne and a house that smelled of fish pie and oyster croquettes, orange peel chewed and savored before tipping the Turkish coffee, teas with his mother and local artists, literary friends—some of whom got drunk on wine and slept on thick futons covered in batiks. His mother baked sweet barley cakes dipped in thin molasses on Easter, rich cardamom sticky buns topped with carrot curls at Christmas, chocolate torte to mark the new year. His father fermented honey mead and on hot summer evenings invited scads of people to sip and tell stories. The old days from Vienna, London, Paris—wherever the teller of the tale was no longer.

He lost both his mom and dad to consumption, that ancient cancer. Edmonds himself was proven by radiograph to have a small barnacle of it lodged in the apex of his left lung.

He was warned not to smoke or engage in habitual carousing, to enjoy his health while he had it, protect himself with balanced amounts of rest and activity and sun. Not once had he disclosed this to Cherise, because in his opinion there were no worries. Always the possibility existed that the barnacle could dislodge, but more likely it was apt to stay in place and would, in time, in fact, calcify and be done. Edmonds shored himself with vitamin powders and covered his face when the winds came, bolstered the oxygen in his blood with doses of Enos, castor oil, and mugs of teas and potions from Oslot, an old blackfella living back of the petrol station near Heath's Draw, east of Jelico, whose wife Adelle had delivered Piotr and Annalesa.

McMurtrey took a pull of a XXXX beer, pointed it at Edmonds, to which Edmonds shook his head no. You made arrangements with the Clearys, right my man? They've got your two and my Pammie and Marvie? Pammie's old enough to be in charge, but I'd prefer adults around. Never too old to worry about them. Kids choke me up, although I never once saw myself as a family man. Not until Jeanne. Talk about *mates*. She made my frat house seem indescribably juvenile. I'd always considered it the summit of intellectualism and *joie de vivre*. Yes, sir. Now to me, that, at the time, was a family. The family of Men. They were my brothers. I loved them as brothers. But little Jeanne was different. She was more fascinating than ten of anyone else I knew. As I told my old man, if a family is ever what you want out of me, then you better approve this gal, because I'm a goner, and I don't think you'll ever hear that out of me again. The old man *and* my mother took to her, too, just as I did. They knew from experience the sensation of feeling that right about something. They've never been apart, my mother and father. Not for one night. My old man is a man money made more righteous. He *loves* my mother. *Loves* her. Like a kid loves Christmas. Even though she's seventy-six, and he's near eighty and forgetful as cotton, I don't think he's ever looked cross-eyed at another woman. Oh, maybe he may have taken a peek, but only if there was no soul around to tell it. Never another woman for my old man. To be crude, Mother is a looker. Built. Hard as it is to think about your own *mater* in that sort of terms, if you know what I mean.

McMurtrey went on to talk about the day he and Jeanne met, the way they'd planned their kids, the way they'd worked and set aside and invested well enough to get to the point of having a big home and a cabin vacation house in Lake Tahoe and the discretionary funds to have a top-end Jurgens camper trailer shipped from South Africa to the east side of Australia— then buying a first-class auto like a Land Rover, hooking it up, and driving west across a nearly raw continent. For the sake of everybody's education.

The way he earned every dime, even if he was from old money and even if his employer was the old man himself.

Of course, one day it will be mine and all but on paper it is right now, he said. But I'll keep doing it just the way my father has and pay myself a reasonable wage and put the rest back into the business. Maybe that's the part of me that wanted this trip. The part that knows life is going to get busier these next twenty years. Knowing what Pammie and Marvie are in for—hell, just getting through high school, then college—not to mention all the moods and hormones. Plus, I know the day is coming when I won't be so available. In a few ways, it's awful having money. I bet I could go for living like you, Tuor. Building this place from nothing but two hands and a boatload of guts. What do you say? Want to trade? My life for yours? No wife-swapping, you understand, just straight-across—my family's life and money for yours?

Edmonds looked at Russell McMurtrey, wanting very much to give in to the inner contempt he felt for every rich bloke who thought buying his way around the world was the answer to anything. Hard as he and Cherise and people like the Clearys had worked to help bring about this life in this place? But at the last, he swallowed the spit he wanted to bestow on the man.

Ah, I'm sorry, Edmonds, McMurtrey said. Just trying to lighten it up a bit. Seems like I've offended you. I'm sorry, my man. Sorry as an old lady.

If McMurtrey said anything else, Edmonds didn't hear. Padding his head against the doorframe with his water bag, he drifted to another time, another place. It was the Reverse Night Dance at the beautiful green edge of the University of Melbourne campus. Her name was Cherise Alexander, from Switzerland, and she loved lavender because it rhymed with her name. She was slight, lissome, dead gorgeous, and she had invited Edmonds to the Reverse Night Dance. Edmonds' mother had bought him a new suit with satin stripes down the trousers and black, shiny shoes. For his date she mixed twigs of lavender with stems of tiny, white lilies of the valley, their little tulip heads dangling like teats. When Edmonds pointed this out, his mother sucked in her breath and very nearly slapped him across the face, and would have, were it not that Edmonds caught her forearm mid-flight. No more, Mom, he said. I'm too old for it.

His mother sighed, the smell of her evening sherry coming out ahead of her words. And so it is, she said, but I did teach you better.

Then it is better you shall get, Edmonds said, handing his mother the white ribbon that would tie the bouquet to Cherise Alexander's wrist.

Do you have your list of conversation topics? his mother asked. Better safe than sorry.

Crikey, Moms, Edmonds said, looking straight into her eyes. They were the same hazel as his. Her bobbed hair, dark blonde but at the forehead a recent shock of white, drew people's gaze to them. He'd seen it. His mother's eyes were technically striking. She'd never had much for lashes, and her brows were a bit fair, but still she was a looker, and the older he got, the more he saw it. That his father had captured her was his favorite accomplishment, he had no doubt. But Edmonds had stared too long, for he saw there was something new in his mother. Whether it was the look of dread or of forgotten wonderment, he couldn't strictly tell. But the change in her façade conjured a bit of both. True to family habit, he dared not initiate an inquisition. Sorry, Moms. No worries, I've me list, he said, lapsing into the local brogue his parents had tried so hard to keep him from developing. This brought a somewhat mischievous grin to his mother's face, a mix of teasing and affection.

Get to the ball, young man, his mother said.

Edmonds kissed her cheek, grabbed the delicate tissue package holding Cherise's corsage, and stepped into Melbourne's early evening air.

***

He couldn't tell where the bloody hell he was. It was dark. That bloke McMurtrey asleep in the middle seat. *The kids' seat.* His bladder was full to broke. So he eased the door handle, straightened himself, stood in the bush night. The sky was a spectacle. He never could keep track of the designs of stars, but he could pick out the Southern Cross. Edmonds' limbs were crimped and needed shaken out, but the moon was new and the light little, so he didn't dare step any further away from the Vanguard than to be decent. One thing he hated terribly was to come across, in the black of night, one of the many deadly snakes the bush was home to.

He couldn't help but notice his trousers had grown loose. He thought he'd engage Cherise to put a little weight back on him. A few more cakes. Then the memory came that Cherise was gone. *Gone!* It just couldn't be. She *couldn't* have run off with Hand. She just couldn't have. There *had* to be explanation. More than just a flirt or fancy. Couldn't be she had run off *with*

Hand. She might have used him for a lift or he coerced her or something else, but what? What?

His pool of urine had quickly stirred the curiosity of a local bilby, fairly well scaring Edmonds off his feet. His stumble wasn't enough to wake McMurtrey, however, who snored wide and shameless. *Backseat,* the Americans called it. Let them call it anything they wanted, so long as they arrived. Which they had, right in Jelico, pulling behind a factory-made caravan. Edmonds had known it sure as the eyes in his head. Caravans were a big do. He was ready for the influx. Whatever was amiss with Cherise, she would get over it. She'd wince for the loss of him and little Piotr and baby Annalesa and soon enough get home. She'd plant her pots of buds and paint her walls any color she liked, and no one again would ever raise a voice to her, and Edmonds never a hand. Nope. He realized now what a mistake that was, how forbidden it should be to strike a woman. It happened only the once, the smack on her face, and they were new-married, and he was smart enough to know he did it out of his own training, for a palm to the face was his mother's favorite method of discipline, but Edmonds believed it a travesty and akin to treason in a marriage. He saw how ragged broken trust became. How impossible to completely last the two sides back together. Even his dodo of a brain understood. His hand still felt the melon sound of flesh against flesh; eyes yet saw the wet on her lower lashes, the cut pride. He had not recognized himself in that blur of minutes. Once amuck, could that evil ever be put back down?

Of course, telling himself the truth, something *had* got into Cherise of late, more than beyond her usual quirks. First she reckoned it was trees she lacked, so Edmonds planted trees. They wanted for height, but pound them into the dirt he did, with Piotr, toddling behind Edmonds carrying daily buckets of water across the yard to help establish them, cackling like a chook, thinking he was helping his dad. Even though the starts leafed and grew in limb and height, still, no, the trees hadn't made her happy.

He listened to Cherise when she was alone in the bath sometimes. Put his ear against the door and listened to her, hoping to get a clue about this woman he so loved, about what was making her heart crook. This sound-memory of her singing in the tub vanished with McMurtrey's stirring. Edmonds could see through the Vanguard's window the man's brown American hair flattened from sleeping as he shifted suddenly to sitting. McMurtrey looked about the car as if alerted by something in his sleep, finally leaning forward to gaze through the glass into the night. Edmonds waved, at which point the other man unlatched the door and climbed out.

Christ, McMurtrey said, voice rusty. Back is broke.

Had to go, Edmonds said.

McMurtrey opened his fly and turned his back. The sound of his stream was that of beads falling on rocks, so dry and unreceptive was the desert earth. The bilby appeared, this time with a partner. Holy criminy! McMurtrey said. What the hell is that?

They'll grow on you, mate, Edmonds said.

Sheezus, Russell McMurtrey said. Any chance there's coffee up ahead?

Edmonds still didn't know whether he liked this Yank. Not a spot now until Gillagong, Edmonds said. It's not but another hundred and fifty or so kilometers. Still be time for you to drive and for me to claim another wink or two if we quick it up a bit.

Quick it up? McMurtrey said.

Good onya, Edmonds said, folding into the driver's seat. Never you mind. I'll drive a mite, I reckon.

The Vanguard's lamps cut the night into dusty wedges. A pair of roos burst across. Edmonds mashed the brake and double-clutched, narrowly missing a mom with a joey poking from her pocket. The noise of the brake was whispery. Both men sucked air. Edmonds gripped the wheel, McMurtrey an armrest and the dash. Both men shoved their feet to the boards.

The spin caught as Edmonds straightened the wheel, finding purchase with the packed-earth track.

JEANNE ANNE HAWTHORNE MCMURTREY

BY THE TIME JEANNE McMurtrey travelled back to her birthplace in Australia with her American husband Russell, she was getting her hair color from a Clairol bottle, but her breasts remained original. Tipped in skin the color of autumn sumac—the exact shade as her hair—they had been the center of her awareness since the morning she happened into her parents' bedroom and saw her mother's nipple tucked into her father's mouth. This was in the farmhouse in Indiana, the green one with peaked gables and wraparound porch, the one they'd moved into from Sydney the year she turned six. Her family grew corn and tobacco and milked cows on their Ohio River bottomland and made solid money from it.

Throughout childhood, her hair color had been dingy and a bit drab, to her mind, despite hours and days sitting in the sun, spritzing her head with lemon juice for the lightening effect. She also rinsed it in apple cider vinegar, to enhance the highlights. All the girls Jeanne knew at school, as well as the women in her extended family, thought time spent on appearance to be a serious and worthwhile investment. She personally believed it got her noticed, which gave her confidence, which translated to her feeling capable of managing tasks that other people might have more trouble with. In high school, for example, she'd been the top of everything, excelling in literature and grammar, art, music. Served as class president, treasurer, vice-president. Voted every year in the yearbook as most likely to succeed. She'd been the first sophomore in the history of English High School to win the student post in the faculty senate. What it showed, as far as her parents' calculation, was selflessness and a willingness to serve—both true indications of them having done their job done correctly. For Jeanne, she liked the glow that came from accomplishment, from checking tasks off lists, and she loved developing the arguments that made people listen.

Learning the practiced ways of adults also helped when it came to convincing the school board and the principal to acquire at least a few so-called luxuries that to Jeanne were necessary to improve the English High School student experience and performance, such as a basketball hoop and painted grids for four-square. Physical activity, she argued, improved circulation and, therefore, brain function and the ability to acquire knowledge, which was not fantasy, but in truth, those two things she lobbied for strictly because *she* wanted them. She loved basketball and four-square, and so did her best friend Marilee Helms.

She also applied for and received, on behalf of the student council, a small grant to open an after-school study hall with tutors, optional but freely available to all students, a predicament which improved the senior exam score average by six points over the previous record-setting year of 1926.

Then there had been her request to the school board for funds to outfit a girl's tennis team and to buy new typewriters for the steno lab and expand library acquisitions and fund a library intern, a position which came with a dime an hour, which was a near fortune to the lucky junior and senior who shared the job three afternoons a week for an hour apiece. Upon graduation, Jeanne was valedictorian, tasked with the commencement speech, and featured in both regional news and in *The Saturday Evening Post's* yearly feature about outstanding American high school seniors.

The balance of Jeanne's childhood was spent on the back of the John Deere tilling ground for baby tobacco plants and dropping seed corn into tiny hillocks. This work was labor intensive in a satisfying way, yet the time spent made her feel like she was compromising—shouldn't she be doing college prep? Still, she stripped tobacco until her hands bled, spent sunny August afternoons plucking corn ears and dropping them into gunny sacks, shucking feed corn to toss into storage bins for milk cows in winter. Popped pea pods by the thousands to help her mother with the canning, wore calluses on the insides of her thighs churning butter, and splintered her hands paddling it into molds. Took a turn at the milking duties, although that got easier the more electric milking equipment with its red rubber tubing her father was able to procure. He took pride in his Grade A dairy operation because it was their detailed cleaning and maintenance of the milking arena that won him this designation, and because by the time she was fourteen, he was confident enough in Jeanne's ability that he turned responsibility for the milk barn to her. My daughter, the milk farmer, became his mode of introduction. When she talked to him about college counselors coming to visit school, and whether he'd investigate possibilities with her, his tart answer was, *You are needed here.*

She couldn't say exactly why she decided to marry Russell McMurtrey at the particular time she did. By then, out of sheer rebellion, Jeanne had broken loose from the family home and spent two years living in Columbia, Kentucky, attending Lindsay-Wilson Normal School. She adapted to teaching easily, loved living the single life across the river from Louisville, loved the four-room flat-topped brick building in Edwardsville, Indiana, where she landed her first job, loved the smell of lined penmanship paper and the fat pencils her young charges learned to grip. Taught them to admire the calluses their fingers bore once they'd gotten the hang of it. She loved her fellow teachers, the way they gathered to share tea and cookies after school on Fridays, when they talked about the logistics of being teachers. She especially loved that she got to live once again near her best childhood friend Marilee Helms, whose parents owned the propane station.

For as long as her family had lived in the green farmhouse

with the wraparound porch, every few months the big white-tanked Helms' Propane and Farm Supply truck pulled up the lane—early in the morning since Jeanne's family was the furthest out and first on the route—brushing low-hanging willow fronds and judicious honeysuckle tendrils on its way around to the back, where Hubert Helms removed and replaced the oblong propane tank which fired the kitchen cook stove. Her family was lucky to have this apparatus since most of their neighbors still cooked with wood. Jeanne always had the urge to walk up and thank him for the grilled sandwiches and brown sugar pie his propane made possible. Of course she didn't and wouldn't, *couldn't* in fact, because of the all-consuming love she held for Mr. Helms. Even the thought of him restricted her rib cage to where she could barely breathe. A crush long and steep as the staircase running from the root cellar past two floors of living space to the attic which served as her bedroom.

If she stood on tiptoe at the window of that bedroom to look out, she could just see across the knobby hillocks the roof of the Helms' house. Each day Mr. Helms was due to arrive, sun or cold, Jeanne pushed open the window sash and leaned out to wave as he drove up. She loved the dove gray of his work uniform, the way it was separate but still part of his movements, the way all year he wore long-sleeved shirts but in summer rolled back the cuffs. She loved his blond hair, the bill of his farm cap, the way it said *Helms* in curly embroidered script next to an outline of a single flame.

She had seen him enough in town and at the propane office paying the bill with her father to know that this early in the morning that gray uniform up close would still smell freshly ironed. Jeanne thought of Gretchen Helms at the ironing board, sprinkling water mixed with cornstarch, pressing a heated iron against collar points, the yoke, creating creases down sleeves and pant legs. She imagined Mrs. Helms scrubbing floors where his shoes stepped and waxing the table where he placed his hat every evening. Certainly if she, Jeanne

Anne Hawthorne, were Mr. Helms's wife, not one dust mote would greet that hat.

All of this was a deep secret she never shared with Marilee, of course, but they talked about plenty otherwise. Both loved books, movies, and magazines, loved to drive a car for no reason other than to feel the motion and freedom, rolling down the windows to breathe in the limestone-scented breeze or the hot mist of southern Indiana rain, for the sake of commenting on it, for the sake of trying to describe the smell. Marilee was wheat-blonde, her hair bobbed and falling over one eye with the sort of dramatic swoop commonly advertised on boxes of permanent wave solution. Her lipstick always pearl-pink and wet, eyes just the slightest bit too big, too wide open, so that to look at her was to bypass all the rest and go straight to her irises, which were the same shade of silver gray as the slate that formed creek beds in the region. Jeanne loved Marilee because she was full of jokes and inventive ideas for ways to pass time, which often included skinny-dipping in those very creeks or driving to places where men their age might be gathering—one of those outings ultimately leading Jeanne to Russell McMurtrey.

All the tiny Ohio River villages on the Indiana side—Lanesville, Edwardsville, Galena, Georgetown, Ramsey, Corydon—had post offices and little else in 1936. Anybody wanting more than mail and the week's gossip had to hitch a wagon or crank the starter on a flivver and make the journey to town. Town was New Albany, a moderately sized steamboat city with Italianate mansions and a tannery upriver from the Ohio Falls, and exactly one mile across the water from Louisville, a journey at the time only afforded by ferry or barge or paddleboat. Of course there was the old wooden K&I bridge, but railroad travel was for the wary. Still the wake of the Depression, petty thieves and pickpockets were as plentiful around Central Station in Louisville as bugs around a flame.

Downtown New Albany was where the region came together for yard goods and sundries and food staples, farm equipment and fuel oil, for the transport markets and shipping and trade, for the occasional talkie, for dime novels, for cherry seltzers, and for the boys to meet the girls, and vice versa. Not until Jeanne was back in Australia, a grown woman, looking into the river-brown eyes of Rich Hand, did she understand how clear and capable a woman she'd become, thanks to having grown up in what for some might be catalogued as a very ordinary life.

RUSSELL MCMURTREY

RUSSELL MCMURTREY JR. lived in New Albany, had gone to Catholic school there, got his degree at Purdue. He was raised in one of the expansive Italianate mansions down by the river and never let anyone forget it: his father owned and operated a dozen or more barges at any given time and was half-owner of the Burley tobacco warehouses throughout Kentucky and was known in both trades as the tightest-fisted businessman on either side of the Ohio. McMurtrey Sr.'s employees were paid weekly in cold cash, and every penny was earned with the burn of muscle and the elegiac stripe of time. Workdays were ten hours at minimum, longer around harvest, and if McMurtrey Sr. hired a person—and he insisted on sizing up himself every man in his employ—it was more less expected the newcomer would take up smoking or chew or at least purchase an occasional cut of plug tobacco or carton of cigarettes, none of which came at a discount, but all of which was available at every warehouse's canteen, which also sold pickled bologna, eggs, and ladles of beans with buttered cornpone. Bringing lunch from home was discouraged, as no provisions existed for keeping food cold, other than what was sold by the canteen. He was one of the first in the region to insist on a payroll savings plan, and maybe the first in the world to put a lock and key on it—those savings accounts required two signatures: one from the worker and one from McMurtrey Sr.'s office in Louisville. Even in the great darkness of the Depression, every man who worked for him came to rest in the belief that the gloom wouldn't last. At very least, if a man's health held, his retirement days would be padded with the dimes and nickels McMurtrey forced him to save, because at the time of employment the worker also would have signed a certificate stating that until such a date—described by McMurtrey Sr. as fifty-one or older—his account could not be breached. Nobody ever dragged him at knifepoint and made him sign sooner. If a man failed to live that long, the funds went to his next of kin and McMurtrey paid for the burial. They're people, McMurtrey was widely and famously known for saying. Thanks to this practice, McMurtrey Sr. had little turnover among his employees. Few were willing to get too far from their pile of coins.

At Purdue, the McMurtrey fortunes were moderate compared to Russell's fraternity brothers, who were spawned from the truly elite. G. Hutchinson's (everybody called him Gee) father held purchase title to every new Ford Motors vehicle east of the Mississippi. Enoch Epperson's family claimed most of the B & O Railroad. Hanley Pitt's father's family operated a little concern called Woolworth's and otherwise for generations had imported textiles from places barely imaginable to most Indiana farmsteads, and was on his mother's side a Vanderbilt. Brock Madison was just as his name indicated—a presidential Madison with James being the least influential as far as the family was concerned—British parliamentarians contributing much more to the power and financial steadfastness of their dynasty than any mere US president. It was Brock with his tailored coats, creaseless shirts, and servant-shined boots who carted Russell to downtown New Albany that day, and Brock who had a hankering for a soda and a hot brown.

Too much cheese and salty ham for me, Russell had said. I'd rather be sipping an Oertel's 92 and yanking pull tabs.

Brock pushed Russell through the Woolworth's screen door. A bell's tinkling announced them. You have no class, he said. See? Look over there. What did I tell you? One apiece just waiting for us. I'll cover the blonde. Busty smart-looking one with the mousy hair is for you.

The two girls were seated at the counter with bottles of Coca-Cola in front of them, chatting with the clerk who was trying to drop peanuts into their drinks. Come on, the young man was saying, just try it. It's the rage. You'll love it.

His white shirt was embroidered with the name Tommy above the right pocket. His dark hair had early gray streak at the temple, curls flipped up around the edges of his pointy service cap. All three had turned toward the bell. Then the whisper from one of the girls, just loud enough to carry, It's Russell McMurtrey and Brock Madison.

The second girl whispered, Holy goodness.

Russell and Brock hitched their pant legs in unison as if practiced, eased into high-backed benches across a diner table from each other. Brock lifted a finger toward Tommy.

Gents, Tommy said, hands in the pockets of his service trousers jangling what sounded like keys and coin. Whatcha havin?

Afternoon, Brock said. Cherry soda and a hot brown for me. Can't speak for my friend.

Russell turned around to look at Jeanne and Marilee and said, Whatever they're having.

***

Russell and Edmonds caught up with Rich and Cherise just outside of Gillagong. Gillagong was from all appearances barely a rest stop for people heading northwest. A roadhouse. One actual hotel. A beer pub. A taxidermist, which seemed oddly out of place, but, as Russell learned from Edmonds was kept busy by those hoping to erect a boar in their living rooms or to make a blanket—a rug, as the Aussies called it—from a kangaroo pelt. The region apparently had once been given to sheep stations dozens of miles square, some owned by Brits who hired squatters and station managers to farm what they could, shuttle sheep on what they couldn't, in the end a great portion of effort for whatever money was made. By 1963 decades of drought had caused most to beg off and let the land go feral. When the rains did come back, there'd be plenty of Hand's type, who'd take work wherever they could get it.

As they pulled into Gillagong, Russell thought about Jeanne and her sweet, school-teacher, farm-girl aristocracy, which was the thing he loved about her the most, but which caused her to hold herself back from so many things, including attraction to any male other than her husband. He could tell she had crossed paths with someone she fancied, and if he were honest with himself, he'd have to say he hired Rich because he wanted to tempt her. Sitting in the Land Rover day after day, he liked feeling the heat rising from her, traveling its scented path into the back seat where Hand sat to one side of Pammie or Marvie, or sometimes in between the two. Russell could feel Hand's instincts routing themselves along the trace Jeanne was sending out. He wanted it for all of them, wanted the tension that filled the car and the decrepit lodge rooms at night, the heft and heave of Jeanne's breasts as she purged herself of this energy onto him, riding him like a whore, both of them hearing the loudness of Hand listening from the opposite side of the wall. He wanted to pick her up naked and carry her to Hand's room, pound on the door, throw her on the bed, and then watch. Watch her open her legs, Hand's face raising a dark brow to the question, Russell nodding the affirmative, Hand stripping off his shirt to a hard-muscled back, then burying his face between her still-solid thighs. Russell longed to do this to Jeanne himself but could not bring himself to describe it to her, let alone initiate the act.

No, Russell hadn't minded at all when Jeanne had told him about making a whore of herself with Hand. It seemed right for reasons he couldn't explain, outside of his own buried desires. He guessed he hoped she learned something she'd want to try on him. He mentioned that very thing, purposefully arching his eyebrows as if in question. In response to which Jeanne had slapped him.

You are okay with this? she'd asked, in that do-it-or-fail school teacher voice of hers. Are you hearing me? He didn't rape me. I brought it on. I know I did. I let him. I wanted it. No knowing why, but I did.

Oh, I heard you, he said, then pushed her into the wall, fumbling with his button and trouser zipper.

I can't, Russell, Jeanne said. Please.

You only think you can't, he said. He held Jeanne in place with his body, nearly a hundred pounds larger than hers, pinned her wrists above her with one hand, nearly spraining his wrist trying to unpack her resisting thighs with the other.

In the beginning, Russell had meant the travel vacation to afford the children a view of their mother's birthplace, of a type of land and a people they'd never seen. Jeanne had been of mixed minds, wanting to see where she had originated, but she was also in the habit of making excuses for not going on his excursions. She maintained the position that they had an obligation to keep their children to a schedule, to prevent excessive stimulation. Russell, however, was raised by a mother who thought nothing of carting her clan off to the seashore or Mardi Gras or the Alps, where Jeanne seemed content helping the children advance their schoolwork or drawing flowers on her canning labels or sewing shirts and dresses for Pammie and Marvie and drapes for the many windows in their home. Conversely, perhaps because of the restraint with which she comported herself, she gave off an energy, like an idling locomotive, that made him smolder for her. In motion but the depths are still, Brock had said not too long after that day at Woolworth's, the lunch that began everything, that marked the fork in the road of Russell's life, the one that led to his being a family man instead of an international playboy, which had otherwise been his only plan. He thought life with Jeanne satisfied him because he imagined her in another incarnation as a madam or somebody's secret mistress—she had that kind of self-possession—yet she still seemed pure. Russell admitted to himself that *he* was done holding back, wanted her as if she were a whore, decided in that instant to let the craving for what he previously could not bring himself to request consume him and lead the charge.

Then at the point of thrusting himself into her, he stopped. He was no rapist. He was not going to make his wife into his victim. He reminded himself that Hand had made her victim enough. He pulled himself to stand, straightened his shirt and refastened his belt, sat on the edge of the bed, wiping sweat from his face, reaching to smooth the salty wet from Jeanne's. Where is he? he asked. Which way is Hand?

Jeanne's voice caught. He took Cherise. Mrs. Tuor. To Gillagong and then up north. She wanted to leave. She was talking about going northwest to Broome, of all places. She wanted to leave her husband. Jeanne dabbed a hankie against her forehead. Russell, I want you to do the thinking about this because I can't. What if there is a baby? And—what if it was our own? There'd be no true way to know. Don't tell our children. I want our life to stay as it is. I do, and you do, too. Don't you?

Jeanne buried her face in a hankie. It was a party, is all, Russell said. We'll think of it that way. A party out of control. And we all get to go home.

Russell reached to embrace his wife, winced to see the marks from his own violence already rising on her neck and breasts. Let's get witch hazel on those spots, he said. Can't have folks talking. Have you got some high sweaters?

Jeanne's disgusted look said he had missed something obvious.

Oh. Right, he said. Packing for this crazy heat. How about cover-up? Don't you sometimes use a makeup stick? Or a scarf?

RICH HAND

THEY WERE THE MCMURTREYS. Russ, Jeanne, Pammie, and Marvie. Pammie and Marvie were cute, inquisitive tykes. Rich Hand was hired and paid to lead them across the continent from Sydney to Perth, a trip few had made without regret.

Rich—full name Richard Charles Bogann Hand—was a common Aussie mix, descended from England's early nineteenth-century brand of criminal (equal the punishment whether the offense was slight or murderous) and the curious and service-minded who hoped to shake a few shillings from the hard fates of others. Even a little pickpocketing was enough to get even the youngest waif boarded and bound for the interminable and often deadly route to New South Wales. Too, Rich's bloodline had on his mother's side a contingent of blackfellas—herself a mulatto—dark-skinned, sponge-haired, flat-nosed keepers of the bush. He was proud of what he came from, and like most of his mob, abhorred the centuries of Pommies shearing people off for sport. One of his dead pap's gray old mates told the story, reckoning aloud that at nearly twenty-six years of age, Rich was old enough to hear a little-known truth about his Da's family.

As the tale went, there was an African blackfella, a Moor, a grandfather several times back who escaped white slave traders trying to steal him off the docks in London by stowing himself between two large parcels just before they were rolled along the plank into the hold of a ship. The old chap described the clanging of the chains holding the ramp, the British aroma of the sea, which was dank and smelled of aging fish in comparison to the fresh salt and lovely tropical blue smells of Sydney Harbour at the time—in such a way that Rich could visualize the scene. The Moor was a town black. Nobody from his family had lived on the dark continent in more than a hundred years. All had been servants to one particular London family: the Marches. Silk, spice, tea. Importers for whom the grandfather's family on his father's side had worked for generations.

Sad thing was, the ship he'd accidentally jumped also had a human cargo destined for the paddocks at Botany Bay. He got mixed in and had his right hand chopped off as a reminder of his supposed crimes. Others—men and women—were rolled over a barrel for a line of sailors. Some lost a foot. Took the cat-o'-nine stripped naked in front of a laughing crowd. Rich could hear the searing iron in the telling of the story; smell the cauterizing of flesh. Heard the yelps of the locals selling necklaces of human ears, purses made from breasts.

You be a good boy, now, and I'll leave you the left one to prick yer missus with, the lieutenant was supposed to have said, just as he stamped the Queen's seal on parchment declaring Rich's ancestor's Christian name—and all he sired—as Hand.

So far the blood mix had served Rich in ways he couldn't have predicted. He didn't know what it was about his looks or comportment, but the daughters of Sydney's social elites couldn't get enough of him. Hair black like an oyster. Cobalt eyes of his mom. That's what he saw in the mirror, same as hundreds of other chaps. It was true his middle-weight frame bore up braids of muscle the color of sawn cypress, and anybody flinging a fist in his direction soon discovered it wasn't blood that powered his veins but pure coal steam. At least that's what it felt like to him. That was the power of his anger on himself. He had knocked one man dead with a pair of blows to the skull, the two having come to fisticuffs at a town party over a sheila, of course, Rich only escaping a trial and imprisonment because the man he killed was a part-Pom Sydney blackfella detested for the way *he* charmed the city's female aristocracy, specifically the prime minister's consort. The incident brought unwanted attention to the string of glittery parties leading up to that particular night with the PM's perfumed wife being dubbed Marie Antoinette on national news. A number of world-famous politicos and movie stars were caught dirtying the edges of the same silk-sheeted beds. Orgies, was the rumor. Sex lives of politicians and celebrities were not normally of concern to the Australian populace, but the idea that a pair of dark-skinned "service" men might be privy to state gossip at a time when war was on everybody's mind turned out to be tantalizing, especially to readers of *The Sydney Gazette.*

Nobody paid much attention when a blackfella came up missing, which was the case after Rich's square off with this one. The story simply died with the man and no query was ever made by the constabulary or journalistic reporters.

In the wake of it, looking to vanish for a bit, Rich Hand hooked himself to this family of Yanks, the McMurtreys. In truth, he signed on mostly for the missus, of course. He caught a whiff of her as she perused the window of a confectioner's shop. Slight sheila like you have a sweet tooth? he said.

Burn it off like a torch, she said. Lucky for me, since my husband likes sweets and likes to share them.

Her hair caught the sun such that she was in halo. He almost said it aloud: *Her hair caught the sun in a halo.* It was tucked into a bit of blue felt and net. She barely missed five feet, her bosoms clenched together behind a shiny sheath in another shade of blue, just off from the color of her hat, two bowls of feminine flesh, pushing against the material with every breath. That was her draw.

But she also looked smart.

Fine day, isn't it? Russell McMurtrey strode up and put one arm around his wife, shooting his other one forward in a solidly American handshake, sun-bleached hair just as stare-attracting as the woman's brunette. I saw you, he said, speaking to the concierge last night, inquiring about a job. He was, Jeanne. I thought about mentioning it, but didn't. This might be a strike of good fortune. If you know this country and can put up a reference and are still open, let's find a place here and talk. We're pulling a caravan across. First time it's been done. If you can't do it, maybe you can recommend somebody or point me to someone who can. The man I originally hired took the deposit and is vacationing in Fiji, I understand. Don't blame him, but I need to replace him.

Russell McMurtrey talked like he was trying not to over-emphasize himself, as polished people usually did. Taller than Rich, broader, his American middle pushed against his shirt quite the same as Jeanne's bosoms pushed from inside her blue sheath. By God, Jeanne, this is luck. Son, we've got this vehicle we bought in Sydney specifically for this trip. The Jurgens Chromebody we had shipped straight from the plant in Johannesburg. Caravans, I've been told you call them. We've planned a journey along the southern route to Perth, aiming to cut northwest and catch this new parking station we heard about. It's supposed to be situated just as you head into the worst of the bush. Yes, I know how far it is. The roads are not paved; some are dirt. It's hot. Gasoline is far apart. and we can't stay in certain places because of heat and laws and the locals. It's possible we could get lost or die of heat and dehydration and never return. There's snakes. Bad people but good people, too. Believe me. I've studied it all, and I've heard it all. Told and retold. But we're intelligent people. Sensible. We've got plenty of water storage and a john and holding tank. Must be somewhere in the vast Outback to drop our mess now and then. Bury it. Propane cook range. Beds. The ease of home. We want our little ones, Pammie and Marvie, to have this trip as an education. Better than an entire year of schoolbooks. Authentic experience. I hear the road's cut through. Rough but cut through. We have orders to check with the local law now and again. People will be watching for us along the way. We're supposed to talk to a reporter by wireless here and there. Take photographs. What do you say? I'll pay fair. We'll make history together, my friend.

Rich looked Russell McMurtrey full on and saw it. Saw all of it. Saw himself tussling with that blue sheath next to the new Land Rover, near this caravan park. (*Just a Day's Drive NW of Denton! True Bush Experience!* said the newspaper advertisement McMurtrey had shown him). Saw the dark storm.

Then you know the bush could kill the mob of us, Rich said, lips working against a smile, then a laugh he couldn't help. The bush snaps when it's pissed, he said. Just like a sheila.

Hell, son, Russell said, pumping Rich's grip and forearm as if to extract water. We're all disposable. That's the beauty, now isn't it? What is it your ruralites say? *Fair dinkum?*

***

A few weeks later, it was all over.

He felt the two men before he saw them. Rich had hired a driver and was loading into an aging black Hudson Cherise's satchels and his pack, plus a pair of shopping bags full of items for the road—toiletries and biscuits and jerky, an expensive pair of star fruits Cherise insisted on. *My mom used to buy them, you see? You want scurvy now do you?* Rich didn't quite hear her; his mind was glazed over by the recognition of what it meant to be a man hooked up to a woman. Not just a party.

What jarred him was that the other bag held a woman's supplies for sponging leakage from her bosoms. He'd been thinking of the situation as temporary. The missus might be ravenous and a joy, yet he was only giving her the full-bore treatment because he knew it would reach an end. She'd miss her kids and want to go home. In the meantime, Rich obsessed over the round volumes of her upper body as if for sustenance, not thinking about the fact that his activity was making her problem worse. She'd whispered to the merchant who'd supplied herbs meant to dry her milk. Rich protested—he in truth enjoyed the fact that the predicament turned daily life sticky and wet, but Cherise insisted on drinking the tea. Kid's milk, not a man's, she said. No kid, no need for milk. She was certain that once they got up around Kuyunga, where the heat was piped direct from Hades, neither of them would be up to the smell of soured mother's milk on her clothing. Rich finally gave in, supposing it true enough.

Beyond that, they kept their purchases small: a pair of toothbrushes, shaving soap.

As it happened, Rich saw Russell McMurtrey before either McMurtrey or Tuor saw him. That didn't take long, now did it, mates? Rich had time to say, before McMurtrey leapt to plow a rolled fist through the Gillagong air. Rich's jaw and teeth felt shattered as cold clay, the impact and shock paralyzing the rest of him. Blood erupted in slow motion as his head stayed solid against the impact, splattering back on McMurtrey, patterning the man's chest in red lace, the feel of it on Rich's own chin and neck like lacewings. He heard Tuor's loud voice exclaiming in the distance, through the plumped-up roar in his ears, just as McMurtrey's second punch made purchase, this time to the side of Rich's head, after which he dropped involuntarily to the ground, cornered between the Hudson's open back door and doorframe.

Give us Cherise, bloody drongo. Are you pickled, Mate? Think a man wouldn't kill to keep her? Tuor's voice said, again as if from a great, wobbly distance. Where is she? Rich tried to shield himself with arms and hands from McMurtrey kicking at his torso and groin. The taste in his mouth impressed him as wasteful, like dropped meat.

Edmonds! The sound of her voice told him the party was over. Edmonds Tuor, you lay back. You lay back or before God I'm tossing it straight at your head.

A bloody cement block. Cherise was holding a bloody cement block over her head.

She'll do it, Mates. Don't doubt it, Edmonds said.

The men stopped, Russell and Edmonds bent at the waists, hands on knees, breathing hard, wiping blood, saliva. Cherise standing on the sidewalk, hands and arms stretched straight overhead gripping a foot-wide cement block. The kind a person might put in a city yard as a decorative component. Toss it to the side, hard, Edmonds said. Slam it to the dirt and get it out of your system. We've already likely raised the constable, so no harm there, and you'll feel better.

Rich watched Cherise, standing for that long moment in the sun, the board sidewalk beneath her. Bystanders gathered. His tongue ridged his broken teeth. Two, he thought. But when he spat the remains into his palm, clearly there were three.

Now you know why some *blokes*, as you call them, end up with gold caps, McMurtrey said, showing the whites of his full set. Rich stood, hanging on the ute door for support, swung at McMurtrey, misjudged the space, landed hard on his knees, then struck his head on the wooden edge of the gutter.

Afternoon, mates.

Rich and the others turned to the dark shorts and gold star of a muscular, uniformed officer. Quarrel with the missus? he asked. Reckon you'll be on with it? The constable's slouch hat hung down his back, its leather lace knotted at the haired point of his neck where he obviously stopped shaving. He was broad-shouldered and reddish-haired with freckles on every inch of visible skin. Chatcolet, his tag said. Rich thought the man came across as a decent sort.

All right then, the constable said. Carry on. The little pond of onlookers parted to make way for him, nodding as he passed. Rich half expected another copper or two to shuffle out of the butcher's or the dry goods to haul them all to lockup, but none did. Soon as the officer was beyond the crowd, the group closed back in, returned attention to Rich, hands and knees on the dirt, the puddle of his blood blackening, and Cherise, and their two adversaries.

PART III

PIOTR TUOR

PIOTR WAS THE FIRST to see the shiny-new tan Land Rover turn up the Outbound's lane on that day in November, 1965. He could see the silhouettes of two adult humans through the auto's window glass—the obvious bloke in the driver's seat, the obvious sheila on the passenger side. The November sun blazed on the entire scene, turning the auto's windows into blinding reflectors as it drew close. Of course, he had no way of recognizing the two, no way of remembering that, as a toddler, he had seen his lovely mom in the clutches of the dark man who had accompanied the couple on that first stay in the caravans. A time in Piotr's life when he was awake and aware of subtle changes in the adult energies around him but lacking the means to communicate about or comment on what he observed.

Then, too, a few days later, a tighter, riper version of this auburn-haired now-arriving missus entwined against a gum tree in the side yard with that same darkish-skinned bloke. Entwined like they were trying to rout something out of each other.

Seeing the two made him fall crook. Crook in his belly. It didn't happen until later that night, but it happened. Watching the silhouettes of them two was what started it all. Same bloated, monster-in-the-closet sensation he felt when Pops told him Mom was taking off on her own, that she wasn't to be living at the Outbound any more. The same beads broke out on his forehead. The same sucking for air. The same taste of the evening's tucker at the back of his throat, attempting to upset itself. Now, however, this time, along with it came the bulbous structure in his groin, the uncontrolled swelling which usually preceded the demon Cutter's appearance.

He knew, of course, from overhearing the previous day's

talk between his sister, Annalesa, and Pops that the subject and the problem for everybody was these two arriving Yanks, Jeanne McMurtrey and her husband Russell. That years ago they created enough of a ruckus to keep people whispering about it all this time, but still yet blokes didn't want to be physically reminded of events by seeing the actual perpetrators. He watched Annalesa approached the ute. Less than a year younger than Piotr, she had become, as he now clearly could see, a woman. He recognized the rise of his mother's chin and squared shoulders as Annalesa crossed the courtyard, saw the mite of power and pride well up. His sister had turned to a beaut of a sheila. More or less, it seemed to him, over a matter of nights.

Piotr strained to hear and try to decipher the language being exchanged between the three of them. The bloke threw his hat to the ground in a way that looked like he meant to slam it, except that a hat to the ground by laws of physics wasn't going to have the impact the man might have hoped for. A fact about which even from across the yard Piotr could tell embarrassed the chap.

In response to her husband's limp action—or perhaps in response to life in general, Piotr couldn't tell—the missus held her hands to her face, turned her bum around and sat it back on the passenger's seat, which caused a puff of dust to arise from the impact of her shoe heels, followed by a very delicate aging-sheila sort of sneeze. The brand where she is trying to prevent herself from jiggling.

Pops never did budge from his place looking out the kitchen window, but Piotr could feel the intensity of whatever pain the old man was suffering. Had to do with Mom, he knew for fact. Bloody prawns showing up with no notice, Pops had said the night before. No time for a bloke to prepare his head.

Annalesa and Pops' murmuring, punctuated by varying levels of insistence, could be heard coming from the dinette long into the night. To Piotr, awakened by it from his new sleep station on the floor of the lounge room, the sound was as if Mom had returned.

***

No sooner had Annalesa and Pops trailed down the hall to bed and Piotr himself dozed off than a man's loud voice echoed from under the lounge like it was arising from a cavern, a voice layered with fast clicks. This had been happening on a regular basis, and terrified Piotr, but he couldn't make himself return to his old sleep spot in the room he'd long been sharing with his younger brother Martin. He found it increasingly difficult to be around Martin. His brother stunk, bluntly put, as he'd given up his weekly tub right when Mom left. Also, Piotr found himself more and more feeling jealous of Martin—of his black-haired looks, his focus on books and bugs and rocks and exploring the elements of wildness. Of the way he got up and went to work cleaning house when Mom left, as if vacuuming the lounge might summon forth the secret remedy to the family's plight.

The sound of the bloke's breathing was like a pinwheel with a pinched cotter pin—it clicked and clicked, same as his voice. Piotr thought of the creature's name as Cotter because of it. A mite of genius, he thought. Poetic. Just now Cotter lay beneath the lounge breathing and giving off his rusty scent, which was like parsnips boiled overly long. Truth told, Piotr had smelled Cotter's rotted odor long before Mom nicked off. It was likely her tender presence that kept the bloke invisible. But now Cotter reigned the household entire, Pops included. The mob was soon apt to know it, too.

Piotr marked his territory by pissing around the perimeter of the house. He found it to be the only thing that kept Cotter away. Evidently demons didn't like human urine. He aimed his first piss of a morning onto the path back of the house near the old gum tree because it right away protected a main way into the place, but he also liked the odiferous impact of the rising sun on it.

One day late in the heat of December, several years after his mother left, Piotr finished his piss and walked around to the play yard, thinking to while away a bit of time on the swings, when a man-shape unblended from the shadow of the shearing shed, the side with the painted castle, long forgotten, the cloth moat melded with the red Outbound dirt. The bloke looked mythological, as if from the pages of a class at Peabody District School: muscled legs ending in bovine hooves, the upper torso smudged between man and smooth-skinned beast, deltoids the size of horse flanks, ending in the head of a ram, the entire thing dark-red shiny and glossed, more brick than brown. Piotr, just turned eighteen, recognized him at once, and Cotter grinned back, the shine from his teeth sending out rays like those of a road train through the dust on the Drury Road. Good onya, mate! Piotr yelled, running down the path to the shed. Good onya!

Cotter's grin grew blinding.

Pops! Quick! Come quick! The bloke's here! Crikey! The bloke's come out from beneath the lounge! He waited for Pops, who stepped onto the porch clad in only his dungarees, shaving mug in hand, looking toward where Piotr was pointing.

Nothing but the sun in your eyes, boy, Pops said.

He's here! He's here! Cotter's here! Piotr said.

Son, have your cuppa, Pops said. You'll wake the tenants.

Bloody prawn. Bloody hell, Piotr said, flinging his now infamous middle finger.

Piotr, there's naught to see. Come to brekky. Get yourself into your bloody britches, Pops said, shaking his head and turning back to the house.

At that point, Piotr initiated a wail to bring the whole of Outbound Caravan Park onto its little porches. The pitch stabbed at the hollows of his head like the womanish screech of a captured boar. It felt good to get it out, coming from a place low and innate the way it did, a tender spot tucked out of sight but begging for salve, the sound searching for, then blending with, the hissing steam around Cotter.

I'm going to kill you! The words formed from disorganized music thrusting from Piotr's throat. He looked to Cotter for explanation.

The demon tented the fingers of his hand over where his heart might or might not be housed. Who? Me? he mouthed, then leaned back in a metal howl surpassing the tenor and grate of Piotr's earlier one.

Piotr? Piotr? Pops sobbed from under the portico, dropping his shaving mug. Sweet Mary and Jesus, boy, he said, pulling back into the house.

He's going to call the coppers. Piotr *felt* rather than heard the whispered words coming from Cotter, as he was not close enough otherwise.

Hesgoingtocallthecoppershesgoingtocallthecoppers. Cotter's voice had taken a singsong rhythm. Piotr was amazed by the quality of it, metal-on-metal turned to vibrant, operatic baritone. *Kill him! Kill him!*

Piotr turned to watch his dad's vanishing ass. Pops? Piotr said. Kill Pops?

In the next instant, the demon was standing stark in front of Piotr, his hellish color changing to midnight blue and undulating. *Tsk. Tsk,* he said, shaking a knuckled finger, then scooping Piotr between the legs, gonads against pelvis. Cotter's smell had intensified to the undeniable stench of sulfur, of aging sheep dung, of unlit petrol. His charcoal lips open, tongue dripping blood, the cavity was now void of teeth. Cotter hoisted his handful heavenward, Piotr wavering and spiraling his arms, teetering as if on stilts. The sky darkened to boiling, and an awful wind sucked Piotr from Cotter's hand into its lips, shaped the sucking shape of Old Man Wind, depositing him skidding under the canvas portico and onto the porch. Piotr wondered briefly what the scene looked like from Pops' vantage.

His skin felt sheared, bleeding and split. He lay back, staring at the green-tinted portico, its waves radio-like, transmitting thoughts to sounds: *this little piggy this little piggy this little piggy*. The shotgun, he figured. He'd get the shotgun and blow Pops' head off. In an instant he fell crook, beset with that same awful queasiness, and he couldn't quit blinking his eyes for the smoke. Lightning then struck the gum tree, split it in two, sparks taking hold in the spice grass near it.

Then the rain started. Straight out of nowhere.

And rain, fair dinkum, if it came to Jelico at the end of December, was apt to be on them for a spell.

JENNY KAY ELIZABETH EVERBACH TUOR

THE NEWSPAPER CALLED HER Tack Girl, in an article titled, "Tack Girl Joins the World." It was Burnt Mine, Montana, 1946. Jenny Kay Elizabeth Everbach was news. She had all the advantages of a loved child in a close community, the disadvantages of poverty and isolation. Her mother was Durinda, father Paul, siblings Philip, Debra, Kathleen, Jennifer, Stephen, Vincent, and Paul Jr., born in the reverse order from the way their parents like to list them. Burnt Mine was pale, sandy, and still. A somewhat colorful poet once mused about what a beautiful place it would be if a bird ever thought to shit a seed on it.

She's healthy, but little, young Dr. Boone said of Jenny Kay when she arrived months early, a red-blue bag of bones and flesh, all gums and bleats. Burnt Mine was a long way by unpaved road from a hospital, but Dr. Boone kept office in Sullivan and didn't mind the drive. His bills came with a yellow note card marking the extra charge for gasoline, the payment of which was entirely voluntary. Most folks followed him to the filling station and gassed his car before he headed back to Sullivan, saving him the task of writing the little card. He always left home on a full tank to prevent folks from overcompensating him.

Jenny Kay did not know about the months she spent tacked to a wall in a cradleboard until 1966. She was twenty and the woman was Melinda Panepinto, a lay therapist in her fifties who rode a bicycle instead of driving a car and whom Jenny Kay had met in journalism class at the U of Montana. They had coffee at Callie's, a bookseller's alongside the Clark Fork River. Melinda read astrology charts and tarot and practiced a therapy known as *amplification*, a treatment mode placing relevance on patterned behaviors.

Amplification sounded to Jenny Kay like snake oil, but Melinda didn't come across as dishonest or untrustworthy, rather a woman who knew her stuff. She won Jenny Kay over when she told about a client named Beth who was married to a wealthy businessman who preferred the Stockman Bar to his wife, a woman who was not without appeal. He was, without telling her prior to their marriage, turned off by her failure to shave her pubis and the way she wore her long hair parted down the middle and twisted it around her fingers when she got nervous, which she did every time he bugged her about shaving. In his words, he didn't like European or hippie.

Beth's true nature was more European and somewhat hippie-leaning, she had told Melinda, but her husband wanted her to dress like women did in magazines, with make-up, nylons, and coordinated outfits. He wanted her to wear short skirts when she preferred jeans and scarf skirts. He insisted she was crazy and regularly arranged physician appointments for her, which she refused to keep because she didn't see anything wrong with herself. She was raised by her unconditionally-loving parents, was used to expecting that treatment, therefore didn't grasp where he was coming from. Beth dropped in to see Melinda because the sign on her door mentioned astrology and tarot, it was only three dollars an hour, and whoever the woman was, she wasn't a shrink.

Melinda told Beth about amplification, instructing her to repeat in an exaggerated manner any movement she felt compelled to, at which point Beth immediately and unconsciously began twisting her hair. Melinda asked her to exaggerate further, but she refused.

Do you mind if I replicate it then? Melinda had asked her, twisting in violent, cranking turns the ends of her own hair, so hard and tight she had to control her own wince.

Beth, glaze-eyed, watched Melinda do this for a long period of time. Melinda didn't stop twisting her hair, and Beth didn't stop staring.

Oh God! she at last cried out, as if erupting, rocking, sobbing, keening, arms across her chest the way a mother might cradle an infant.

When ages later Beth finally was able to sit up and speak, Melinda went off to get a cold cloth. As she explained upon return, ice in a wet hanky had a forceful effect on people as they were coming out of an amplification session. It was the equivalent of jumping in a snowbank after sitting in a sweat lodge. It fine-tuned by startling the senses and bringing long-vanished memories instantly awake.

After a few moments, Beth explained her experience. She had been fifteen, walking down the stairs of her parents' home wearing a midriff top with buttons in the back and pedal pushers. Pink gingham and pink denim. She had bought and paid for the material and sewed them herself for the occasion. Her parents, up to that time, had refused to allow her to date, but Eddie Lindsey from economics class at Littleman High School had asked her to take in a movie, and she had been sassy and belligerent about going. It was, she had argued, just the Roxy in downtown Montgomery, Alabama, where she had been raised and her family had lived since she was a kid. Nobody else saw any harm in letting their kids go to movies. Why was it only her parents who did?

She raced to greet Eddie at the front door, but her father beat her to it. He saw the boy and registered the way she was dressed nearly at once, then went berserk, shouting and grabbing her by the hair, tearing at the front of her until her back buttons broke.

The brassiere strap gave way, too, and out tumbled her breasts, right in front of her father and Eddie and her mother and her brother, who had come from his room in the basement to check out the commotion. They stood flabbergasted in the stone silence, all except the girl, who was crying, naked to the waist. Eventually Eddie took off his shirt and wrapped her in it, and her mother led her back upstairs, cooing and soothing her.

As for the father, he walked into his den and sat down to read the paper. The girl never talked to Eddie again, but every boy in school razzed her for a replay and certain groups of them begged her for it each time she was forced to walk past them. It became unbearable enough that she had to transfer to another school.

Whether the story Melinda told was true or not, Jenny Kay, twenty years old and looking for direction, couldn't get the scene out of her head and so set an appointment with Melinda.

The office was a tiny storefront. A ring of symbols on the front door with the title in an arc above it: Signs of the Zodiac. Someone had painted Jesus Saves across the word zodiac. Although an attempt had been made to scrape away the rough-script letters, still the shadow lingered. The room was barely wide enough for a sofa, a problem solved by floating it at an angle across the hardwood. Two chairs—one aging wicker, the other floral tapestry in shades of old rose—offset a tufted sofa upholstered in pink mohair. Frosted pink. A woman's design work, no doubt about it, with one wall white-washed brick and the others in varying intensities of sea green. A slow fan spun, suspended from a ceiling still covered with its original pressed copper. Framed black and white prints hung on the wall opposite the white brick. Jenny Kay was put off by the pink, but the sofa was soothing as old pajamas, such that the moment she sat and leaned against the back and sides of it she could feel its magic spell.

She felt herself pulled inward, almost forcefully, into what was obviously a hypnotic state, despite her never having been hypnotized before. *Was there something in that tea? No, wait. Melinda never came back with the tea. Did she?* Nothing visible of the tastefully painted brick, only herself, Jenny Kay Everbach, at the bottom of a mirrored well that left her no choice but to stare at the many sides of herself. Silver mirrors. All around. Deep in a well made up of nothing but silver mirrors.

Melinda only had to say, Tell me why you are here, and Jenny Kay to say, I want to know why I always feel out of place. And Melinda to say, Why do you want to know? And Jenny Kay to say, Because I don't want to feel out of place any more. The fan blades circled. Jenny Kay could sense time passing on the sidewalks, the pulsation of it. Students in their university classes. Cash registers ringing purchases. Fates being decided. Property purchased. People's dental cavities filled. Tourists and locals dashing in and out of coffee shops and restaurants.

After an amount of time passed (Jenny Kay did not know how long) Melinda said, I've never in my life had a backache, but I feel as if I've been standing on brick all night. My entire back is in spasm. I don't know how long I can stand this. I need you to get to where you are going. The pain is incredible.

Jenny Kay felt herself stand, then reel, as if slapped. The sensation ricocheted through her body, causing her to fold at the waist. She lowered her torso, back to the fabric of the sofa, then to the floor, no longer inside the mirrored well. Arms straight and held tight to her side, eyes closed, she felt herself suck air as if it were a thumb.

When she described the sensation to Melinda later, Jenny Kay told how she had been, in that instant, lifted out of consciousness and into a warm enclosure, dark, with a tiny bit of light hovering just beyond her face. She recognized the feeling as cramped and cozy and reminiscent of all the cramped and cozy places she'd ever rented. She hadn't until that moment understood that she always preferred stamp-sized apartments, just as she drove a VW packed to the brim with boxes of belongings for which there was never room in her tiny abodes.

The light coming from beyond the cradleboard's beaded overhang this time was new and distinct. A light that fluctuated as if craving its own disappearance. Jenny Kay waited, watched it with her adult understanding, knowing that a baby version of herself was behind the woodstove, in a cradle hung on a horseshoe nail, warm enough but not too warm, unable to consider reality outside her own silhouette.

At one point, Jenny Kay learned later, she began flailing and certain she had to get out, until a face appeared, a gentle touch, a soothing voice from a mouth that cooed and kissed her. She felt her constraints take on purpose, reminding her that staying wrapped and suspended translated to the face periodically appearing. To this end she kept her eyes focused beyond the cradleboard's hanging beads.

At last the straps began disintegrating, falling in ashes to the ground. Jenny Kay lowered her knees and feet, stood upright, leaning for balance against what appeared to her to be the cold woodstove but was in truth the frosted-pink sofa. Her eyes and lungs throbbed from sobbing, and she felt awash with gratitude, the thumb in her mouth at once strange but normal.

***

By 1973, thanks to an array of events, most of which involved dissatisfying relationships with men, Jenny Kay ended up passing stubbies, as the Aussies called them, and pouring pints at the Tanzey-Davis in the bleak Outback of Western Australia. The town was Gillagong, a day or more from nowhere, which meant the Tanzey-Davis was the region's only watering hole. How the place got its name was a matter of regular discussion. Stories abounded. Which was how she got started writing a column for the *Denton Record*—kept track of the tales and made up her own. Wrote them out one at a time on an old Royal typewriter, sent it to Denton. If the editor liked it, he published it and sent her a dollar or two.

From there it was bits of gossip and news about Gillagong folk, which upped the weekly rag's popularity in both places, since a number of people bought it just for her stories, otherwise the two towns separately didn't have enough occurrences to warrant the printing or purchase of it. Denton, two days' drive, nothing but eight pubs, a supply store, and a resident camel available for the price of a ticket for riding and for tourists to take a snapshot.

There was a larger world out there, Jenny Kay knew. She'd taken the long way across it, learning all her lessons the hard way, the hurt way. By comparison, the rough rooms of the Tanzey-Davis felt much less harsh to her. She was in love with every splinter, not to mention the hand-carved back bar, which for reasons tough to determine made her soul feel free and easy. Maybe in a past life she was a carver. Maybe she was supposed to be a carver in this life, but missed her calling. Rich visionary from Wales ordered it custom-built out of rosewood from the Middle East, accented with burled maple from the US—or so said the letter that came taped to the bottom of its locking cash drawer. Points of discussion included the fact that it had been shipped on a slave boat, came equipped with lanterns meant for burning boar tallow, and the front right end featured a U-shaped bracket holding a large brass gong inscribed in Chinese. On the back on a yellowed sheet of paper was written the supposed interpretation: *Not only fine feathers make a fine bird.* Of course, Jenny Kay hadn't been on the job five minutes before she was declared A Fine Bird. Almost immediately patrons began calling her Birdie.

Yes, she knew she had a mind good for something besides tart retorts to this sheep-brained crew of cane men and shearers, but she adored them and generated whatever mental stimulation she needed by writing her articles, reading books through the book loan-out from Perth (the paper and twine packages arrived every third week) and inventing games and contests for her customers, one of which was in progress. She was calling it Birdie's Panty Poll, and made it clear the results would be broadcast in the upcoming edition of the *Denton Record*. At the least the related jokes ought to help the crowd wait out the rain, which had started falling in steel-colored sheets.

She tacked pages of butcher parchment alongside each other on the staircase wall to create a large grid, one column for Tighty-Whities, one for Under-Alls, one for Skivvies, one for Birthday Suits, one for Ladies' Teddies.

By the time she was done, every name in the room—and some that yet hadn't shown up but likely would—were listed in a column down the left side of the poster. Denton's constable, Merl Chatcolet, sat watching, his mitts around a bitter. She'd lined up his name and marked him an X under Ladies' Teddies, just to rile him. He was brooding over having to truss-coat one of the young men over near Jelico. Twenty-two and the family had been scared shitless of him for the past six years. Merl was vocal that night about how much he hated having to cart mental cases clear to Adelaide now to the bin. Used to be Sisters of Hollywood in Perth took them. Days closer, which was the least of it. Now it took provisions for two transport guards, plus the transportee. Board. A week's board minimum apiece. Hazard pay.

The mom run off, I reckon, Merl said. Other kids was a young schoolboy, a teenager she-hellcat—you could tell—and a dark-haired bloke looked like he might have a bit of blackfella, but a mite younger than the sheila. Three of them, he said, all so close in age you have to wonder if nobody ever told the mom about the basics. Plus a younger joey—I don't know, old enough to wake up with a stiffy, I reckon.

Merl chatted on until he finally talked his way into the fact that it was to everyone's benefit to get the young man out of the house. Rose before porridge, he said, every few months for years now, according to the tenants, wavin' about and blowin' on about some fiery cartoon bloke of a devil. It's been black rain around Jelico territory for a fortnight, no end in sight. The kid has gone off plain balookers, ripping rotten boards off the old shed, trying to build a boat. It's not business for a bloody prawn, not for a bloody prawn.

Jenny Kay leaned on the counter, chin in hand, listening

but not hearing. It was the rain on the tin roof that had her attention. She poured Merl another pint, and then stepped to the open door. It's going to be an awful rain, she said.

Yep, Merl said. Reckon this'll be a big one, Birdie. Hope we all live to tell the tale.

The Big One was a phrase folks in Western Australia used regularly. It had been years since a good, restorative rain. Every half century or so, heaven uncorked its barrels, as Merl liked to put it. When that happened, Deadhorse Creek and Gillagong Slough became a roaring, killing monster, swallowing man, beast, and hearth, rearranging the jagged edge of the sky. You might ride it out in a dory; Merl went on, if a dory were about. A flat-bottomed skiff would be easily overwhelmed if the water was really rushing. Otherwise, the only groundwater around Gillagong came whenever some shearer stopped for his piss, and the flies sucked that up before it had a chance to hit ground, so there wasn't a dory to be had. A few old-timers might keep one stored, like Australian Noahs, aimed to be prepared for the prophesied event. More than a few for certain had inflatables tucked away on a shelf. Merl had seen them himself, as over the years he had had reason to make contact with just about every resident in his wide territory.

You know, Merl said, That's why Aussie men love women with meat on their bones—something to hold onto when The Big One comes.

Jenny Kay punched him in the upper arm. She hated that discussion, not to mention the accompanying epithet: *fat floats*. She often wondered what maniac built a roadhouse in such a wasted place and why it drew men with such minds. Somebody dug a well and figured out goannas made a good stew. Maybe dehydration and malnutrition made them think as they did.

The hour was not yet five, but the rain brought shadows and chill, so Jenny Kay lit lamps and the grill early, laid out haddock and lamb, sliced potatoes into salt water for chips.

They'd be in tonight, the bunch from Kuyunga, even Chilla-roog, a few grimy ones wanting to paw at her, even though all knew she wasn't for sale and sure as balls none was getting her for free.

Merl's tale bothered her. He'd said the young man would be subject to electric currents and insulin shock. She'd read a book about a Kiwi woman named Janet Frame whose two sisters drowned and who was diagnosed a schizophrenic when she was actually a poet who didn't fit the usual mold. Jenny Kay felt kinship with Janet Frame. An outsider's life took its toll on a person. Everybody in Gillagong was an outsider to the place they had come from. Lucky for her, being American, locals and tourists loved to listen to her talk and remark about her Yankee accent. She was a mystery, travelling such a distance and casting her lot among them. The Outback was a language few understood and anyone who thrived in it belonged to a mindset those who arrived there first admired. Plus, Jenny Kay was a woman. Still young enough to turn heads. Most women passing through Gillagong sat on the passenger side of a Holden and fanned their sweat, giving flies the Aussie salute, sick with dust and heat, while their men came inside to pound a pair of tinnies. Jenny Kay endured weather and flies alongside everybody else without complaint. When she turned Merl Chatcolet down for sex the one and only time he ever suggested it, he told her she was a mate of a sheila in a place where sheilas had no place. *A good bird.*

By six o'clock, every rough-sawn table had chairs drawn to it and was filled with plates and the click and palm-splat of men eating and expressing dismay over circumstances, whether that be the rain or sugar cane bottoming now that Parliament was letting *any bloody bloke with two arms* inside Australia's borders. Jenny Kay balanced three plates per arm. She got behind on pints, so Merl started passing tinnies of XXXX, which the crowd tolerated just fine. There wasn't a soul in the place to trust with the taps. They'd swill more than they'd sell.

At nine o'clock she tapped the bell to mark the end of supper and bought the house a round. She enjoyed getting lost in the swift nature of mealtime. Could count on a handful any night, although not often a crowd as big as this. The rain was still bringing them in, too, but less steady the later it got, each new arrival pawing open paper-wrapped meat and biscuits Jenny Kay had made on pure instinct and put aside during the night's few still moments. Eventually it got down to the door opening only once in a while to let somebody out for a breath of air and to gauge the situation, the iron smell of rising creek water rushing in with it. The last to arrive came in stomping off the water, claiming, *it's coming faster than a new groom*. She wrote it down to consider for her next contest—Big Rain Metaphors. Knowing she'd have to explain the concept of metaphor to some.

Around ten bells word came that the road to Kuyunga had washed out. A loud murmur of concern went up. The Tanzey-Davis had maybe six bunks up in the boarding room, in addition to Jenny Kay's quarters, which held space for maybe seven or eight bedrolls. She could sleep in the larder where the doors locked. At ten-thirty she climbed onto a stool and clanged the brass gong. The sound was hollow and reminded Jenny Kay of the way water ripples around a tossed pebble. Somber, too, perhaps even melancholy, but undoubtedly useful, digging a hole in the crowd's energy and sore as a bad tooth.

As for Jenny Kay, she liked the authority the gong gave her. She didn't ring it often, but when she did, it made upwards of fifty hard-rode Outback men stop dead. It was the only time she gave them permission to look at her. She felt their eyes thick as bristles on a boar, taking her in.

Two things, Jenny Kay said, soon as the finger whistles and applause ceased. One, she said, pointing an extended arm and finger at the charts on the wall, Panty Poll.

The roar took up again, along with the clatter of forks and empty tinnies pounding the tables. She hit the brass this time with short rat-a-tats, stilling the transmission with her thumb against the edge. Listen or I'll close the taps, she said, arms crossed beneath her breasts. The crowd funneled into a buzz, then nothing. The drilling rain against the Tanzey-Davis's tin roof was all Jenny Kay heard. *A miracle.*

Second, she said, it doesn't look like the rain will stop. I've got six cots at a dollar and a half. If you don't mind the floor, I've got a few bedrolls, a dollar each. If you want a place to drop your own rug, we'll clear back tables. Breakfast at six, for who wants it. Meantime, sign your name under my Panty Poll. It's required if you're going to be breathing my air.

The men sent up a collective chuckle. How late you pouring? It was Hugh Shevlin, who owned two houses, one in Denton, and an old one he used on holiday up Deadhorse Creek.

We'll shut it at midnight, she said, hell *or* high water.

It'll be hell if we have to sleep with Hugh Shevlin, somebody from the crowd yelled.

The rest moaned slightly as Jenny Kay climbed down from the counter. Better start slinging them rounds then, a voice rang out from the crowd, 'cause if I'm to plant an ass cheek on the planks in the midst of this bloody mob, I'll sure as hell have to be drunk to do it.

The comment garnered a small response, but not enough to infiltrate the applause and snorts of approval as Jenny Kay hoisted to the bar the first in a long night's worth of pints, three to a palm, looking in the rainy dim like a pair of shiny, overgrown paws.

They called it the Wednesday Flood of '73. Jenny Kay's newspaper accounts were framed and hung on every proprietor's wall in the district, featuring tales of heroism, of rescuers setting off into the unknown laden with kerosene, wicks, medicine, and food supplies. One was about Bill Rader, whose house was lost to a mudslide, all but the living room which was left standing intact around Bill who had been fevered, down with the ague, sleeping on the floor between his lounge and wood burner in that very room. One version of the story says he slept right through, only a bit of mud splashing his face. Another says he was too sick to get up, figuring one way or the other to be dead by morning. The same version said he scribed a note on a shred of paper that read, *Anybody taken, let it be me.* A stained note with those words was at some point posted in a public house in Kuyunga, although nobody could get Bill to verify his handwriting.

Another slide nudged Hugh Shevlin's old place. Bill's house and Hugh's were built in river draws dormant since before the Pommies started plucking panhandlers off London streets and shipping them to Botany Bay. The story went that blackfellas tried to warn immigrants off of building in draws, saying, *the water will always be coming,* but the prophecy was forgotten or ignored, both houses well on to fifty years old.

The mud was kinder to the Shevlin house, or the house was too tough, too sturdy, or the wall of mud itself flawed, cleft in the middle by a huge sweet gum root or parliamentary-sized boulder. Whatever the cause, the mud split, one side going one way around Hugh's old house and the other side going the other. Folks from all around drove out to take pictures of the House-That-Could, adorned as if around the neck by a great red fur collar of Gilly mud.

By plane the region must have looked like a split, oozing melon. Jenny Kay climbed to the widow's deck of her station house, giving herself a line of vision across the plains plowed by flowing mud. Enormous boulders had worked their way above ground, roads flowed with water deep as a ute's running boards almost a week after the rain had stopped. Great sweet gums fallen from their own weight, root balls above ground, foreign-looking. Shearing and loading sheds filled with mud, barred by rock. Word got around that Bob and Carol Garnett's station lost all of its corrals, their water tanks—all thirteen of them—on their sides, ruptured, spilling a year's worth of water into a newly formed lake. Their chicken house floated away, along with three hundred laying hens. Bob joked about having called his place Summit Station, thinking its minor elevation enough to avoid even the floodwaters of the distant Drury River or the closer Downbrumby Slough, if they ever came that far. He couldn't have imagined Summit Station's ruin arriving from the sky itself. The Lord giveth. The Lord taketh, Carol was rumored to have said, after which Bob cuffed her, which he was prone to do. Supposedly for the first time Carol cuffed him back and then spat on his shoes.

Jenny Kay heard stories about a commune-type place several hours away from Gillagong where inhabitants had resorted to building lean-tos on the north side of Downbrumby Slough, parking their utes and wagons on shaded south banks, then constructing rope footbridges to cross a flow eight feet deep to gather supplies and necessaries from their stranded houses. Chuck and Diggie Stertz lost their tack hut, as well as an irrigation flume, it was told, house wet to the floorboards, but livable. Lost their fences and garden. Grant and Barbara Warnecke had nineteen inches of standing, muddy water. By Sunday they'd cleaned out the mud, scraped the walls, and moved back in. They, too, lost garden soil but not the woodpile; both got chest colds. When folks suggested moving the house off Downbrumby, Barbara supposedly said, I'd as soon be dead as live any other place.

The Wightmans lost their railroad car. Nobody ever knew how a railroad car came to be near Downbrumby Slough, but it was there when the Wightmans bought the section in '42. They used it as a bunk house for hands. Testimony to the water's force, the metal box tossed around and finally landed jammed against a pair of boulders, west of the confluence of Kallee Spit and Downbrumby Slough, a kilometer from where it started. Both of them later described the sound to Jenny Kay in the same way: *it sounded and shook like there ought to be pieces of sky on the ground.*

Rory and Lana Arnold drew the real short straw, however. They were on the veranda watching the water rise—quick and brown and smelling like plant roots, as Lana told it—when they decided they ought to get to higher ground. The Wightmans showed up at that moment to tell about the destruction of their railcar bunkhouse, suggesting it was time for the Arnolds to pack important papers and head out. Probably no time for anything else. Lana started to cry and just as quick the house began to shake and tremble. The two couples fled up the knoll at that precise moment, breaching the crest in time to turn back and look straight into a surge of water lifting the Arnold's cottage *like a sugar cube on a tongue*, Rory told Jenny Kay, swinging it around, and setting it adrift. The house—veranda and all—eventually hit the Wightman's railcar, slicing off the top two-thirds easy as cake. The rest exploded into sticks and plaster dust on the spot.

They later heard that several caravans over at a tourist place called The Outbound fell into the water at the same time, when the far-east end of Downbrumby eroded the backside of the old sheep station that had been turned into a place to rent caravans for holidays. Luckily the proprietor and tenants were out helping folks over closer toward Gillagong.

Scores of area inhabitants got cut off from aid, including the parson of Beech Methodist Chapel for Aboriginals, who remained by himself for most of two weeks, but who made the news by claiming to be tended to by a band on walkabout. Turned out it was true, and when the clan came back to check on him, he called the local papers and a big to-do was made that ended up inspiring a group of volunteers to repair structural damage to the chapel.

Keith Watters, along with several others, put together a rescue posse and headed out for more populated areas, carrying hand radios, lamp fuel, kibble, batteries, and mail to residents of College Creek vicinity. College Creek's constable Roger Jett was having a grand first week on the job, and praised the efforts of hearty Outback folk and how they made the work bearable. Sally and Davis Tanzey, absentee owners of the Tanzey-Davis, and Jenny Kay's lien-holders, arrived on Wednesday and helped opened the saloon to serve meals—two hundred and fifty the first two days. Gerald Perren, who headed another rescue team, asked that notice be made of the volunteers who had left the comfort of home in Perth: Kate Wheeler, Joe Hallam, Dorothy Daggett, Charles Lebeque, Dorothy Kappel, James Cornell, Lou Ann Jordan, Mike Smyth. The only casualties of life, Jenny Kay's related article noted, were Honey Reese's dog Honeybee, assumed drowned, and Ezra Nobles, who was accidentally shot by Bert Egbert. Ezra had been passing the fourth night of the downpour in the Tanzey-Davis by goading Bert over a girl. The sprawling and laughing got bothersome enough that Jenny Kay sounded the Chinese bell and commissioned customers to toss them both out by the scruff of their shoulders. Patrons for the most part went about their business until the shot rang out, and the entire crowd bolted out the double doors just in time to see through the pouring rain Bert put the second shot from a .44 into Ezra, who had dropped to his knees watching his own blood spread deep enough when mixed with the standing water to float the two spent brass casings. Everyone stood blinking until Ezra dropped over, at which point Bert fell, keening and crying like a baby. It went to the Denton constable, Merl Chatcolet, to escort him to lockup.

DALE MCMURTREY

IT WASN'T ALL THAT HARD to locate a man with Rich Hand's reputation for being at once a roughneck and a ladies' man, even all those years after he'd reportedly stopped working towards creating the reputation. Dale McMurtrey followed his mother's directions to Jelico, then Hand's ancient trail beginning at the Outbound Caravan Park, which was run by an odd man named Piotr Tuor, not too much older than himself and who was supposed to be his half-brother's half-brother. That is to say, Piotr Tour and Dale McMurtrey's half-brother Martin shared a mother.

After that to the town of Gillagong, which was little more than a beer stop. Aussies loved their beer, and he was quickly realizing he'd have to get used to substituting the relatively pale pilsner version for his preferred ales and bitters if he was to drink anything at all, which was how scarce drinking water was. Already he understood that XXXX—pronounced four-ex—was the libation to order if you wanted people to think you knew what you were doing. From Gillagong he hitched a ride back down to a sheep ranch south of Kuyunga, almost a day's ride, and for which he paid the driver two hundred Aussie dollars, dropping his parcels for safe keeping at one of two roadhouses along the way.

Hand was said to cook for an outfitter. Dale had imagined his father sun-darkened and healthy but slightly grizzled, still working for wages, and couldn't picture what trail had led a man of such reputation to end up patting biscuits for wealthy foreigners. For Dale himself, he wasn't that serious about finding the man. Dale was an American with the resources to pick and choose where he might go. He'd thus far avoided matrimony and paternity, words he long ago blacked out of his personal lexicon. The journey to wealth had been eighty hours a week, a liquored thrill ride, until it became riddled with middle-class angst, once he'd seen himself how many brown backs and manipulated psyches had borne the invisible labor of it and how little they shared of the kitty. Dale was trying to compensate by globe-trotting in search of humanitarian projects. So far he'd found a café in a village outside of Tehran with English-course compositions flickering on computer monitors in a pale earth, hand-dug basement classroom, and a network of naturopaths in Kenya providing health care and teaching restorative farming practices while commissioning elders to teach shamanism and traditional wildcraft medicine to young apprentices and to carefully chosen Anglos from Europe and America.

He built a building big enough to hold three classes adjacent to the café, hired a teacher, and sponsored a reading contest, the reward of which was five thousand dollars with which to improve the community. The winning student chose to bring someone to teach them how to keep bees. The clinic in Kenya got a million dollars' worth of additions to their building including clinic rooms and classrooms.

Dale backpacked across Europe and the Middle East, India, hired bush taxis to take him through parts of Africa, recording his adventures in a series of illustrated journals he sent back to his parents in the States and which his mother was typing up to get published. He wasn't angry: he wanted them to know that, but he did depart rather spontaneously on his world tour after the emotional flood that was his mother's *truthburst*, as he had come to think of it. They would blame themselves to their deaths if his life came to its end during his travels. Were it not for glaucoma and a childhood spent carted between specialists, this truth might never have been unearthed. Childhood glaucoma was not completely rare, but rare enough, and hereditary. He supposed if he had behaved as expected, married young, had children, he would have heard the story sooner. As it was, his parents waited until they themselves were worrying over wills and inheritances to call their children home for the conference.

His mother and father, Jeanne and Russell McMurtrey of San Diego, both had the flu at the same time and had grown hysterical over the inevitability of their deaths. Old couples died together in auto accidents on a regular basis, so why not the flu, they reasoned, and insisted all three of them—Dale, Pam, and Marv—converge at their home immediately *sans* spouses or offspring, first class and on the parents' dime.

Arriving at the house the three grew up in, made fresh since with bleached oak floors and white furniture (which their mother *had always wanted but never dared because of you kids*), Dale saw clearly that both parents were going to survive the flu, yet Jeanne did appear spent and listless. In the midst of a dinner of minted lamb and roast potatoes, she collapsed into an emotional, sobbing fit. What a pleasure, Pam had just been saying, to be seated at the dinner table of their childhood home when it wasn't a holiday, Balboa Park within walking distance, and the shops of central Hillcrest. At first flash the outburst annoyed them in the way of *Mom being Mom again*; however, when seconds turned to long minutes, the four of them moved in unison to help her to the living room and to calm her.

Finally, Jeanne caught breath enough to talk. She wove her story in the soft, quiet, unemotional voice she used when detailing unpleasant circumstances. Their father sat with his arm about her shoulders, looking like a pale, snow-haired version of the man who'd raised them. He'd done a damn good job of it. They grew up with money, but his mother and father taught all three to work hard and be grateful. A hard swallow arose in Dale's throat. His father was emotionally limited. He'd never really known it until that moment.

Dale's true father was a man named Rich Hand, his mother said. Russell wasn't his biological father after all. Pam and Marv's, yes. Dale had been conceived in Australia, as they all knew, but by a man who had been hired as their road assistant and tour guide. Dale listened without moving as his mother narrated the tale. A poet would love a story like theirs, he thought. Russell had forgiven Jeanne long ago. A happy end to a hard story. Pam and Marv, who shared many experiences before Dale was born, took it hard, because they remembered Rich, thought him darkly exotic, and had liked him. In the next breath Marv whistled, saying, holy fuck. Do you realize how close we came to not having Dale in our lives at all? Holy fuck, man, at which point he grabbed Dale in his signature bear hug. Marv weighed three hundred pounds, was six foot, eight inches tall, played for the NFL, the 49-ers, offensive tackle. People always looked at Pam and Marv and Martin and made comment. Dale was dark where they were fair. Reticent genes, was the robotic answer, reinforced by testimony of the genealogist Dale once consulted, out of curiosity.

Pam looked at Dale. Too much, she said. It's too much. Rewind. I want a rewind.

Dale felt nothing but a strong sense of reality. No sadness. No regret. No fear. He hugged his mother and father, kissed them on the cheek. You shouldn't have lived with it, Mom. You should have told us. It was never a question. Even if we had known about it, it wouldn't have been a question.

Pam and Marv said similar things.

I was afraid I'd mess you up, she said.

His siblings and parents were blowing their noses into tissues when Dale moved to the sideboard to pour drinks, then excused himself to the bathroom, after which he slipped into his parents' bedroom to retrieve his shoes and jacket, soft-footed it back through the kitchen to the patio, then off into the San Diego night.

Dale enjoyed walking the Hillcrest district after dark, the feeling of people searching, hoping to make connection. Restaurants. Galleries. Artsy shops and import stores. Sometimes he gave into his curiosity about gay bars, half-fearing the sense of camaraderie he felt among the clientele. Dale was not sexually attracted to men, at least none he'd ever run across, but also only once or twice in his life had he felt drawn enough to a woman to even start a conversation. Since bar talk with heterosexual men virtually always drifted one direction, he felt a certain rightness in those places where men felt safe talking to other men about something besides sports and breasts.

A place called Manny's was open. Empty but for the bartender watching public broadcasting. Track lights hung over the bar, a dozen of them, low wattage. The modest amount of light they put out created a bit of calm. Dale downed shots of Jameson's, finally asked for coffee.

What's news? the bartender asked.

Life does us a favor during those long stretches when nothing much changes, he said.

It's a dogfight no matter what, the bartender said, his accent a bit southern.

Like a brick tit, Dale said. A metaphoric brick tit.

Simile, the bartender said. Like a brick tit is a simile.

Dale laughed. Right. Educated asshole like me ought to know that.

The man looked Dale in the eye and said, There's a cure for everything.

Tell you what, Dale said, standing to reach into a jeans pocket for his clip of bills, that's what rain checks are for.

Gotcha, the bartender said, waving off the money, which Dale dropped into the tip jar. You know where to find me.

The street air had been subtle and scented with salt. Somewhere in the four directions were the various throbbing wombs of the US naval stations, the Air Force, the Marines, all awake and busy with wars and invasions. The thought of the continental US flattened and smoking counteracted four shots of Jamesons. Dale wished he used weed, wished he were closer to the beach. But to Rich Hand? Did he wish he were closer to Rich Hand? His father and the cause of his glaucoma was some roving Aussie son of a bitch named Rich Hand? And then to think of his mother, a bright, confident, pure-hearted creature of a woman who had put aside every single one of her own plans to focus on the prudent and conscious rearing of her children, except for the columns she wrote for the *Pacific Gazette* and the *Balboa Weekly* about women's rights and liberal politics.

Since there was no way to know what to make of it, he let it go. He would tell his parents, as Pam and Marv already had, that what he hadn't known hadn't hurt him, nor did what he knew now. Jeanne and Russell McMurtrey were his mother and father. Pam and Marv were his blonde-haired sister and brother. He was dark. So what. He was more interested in knowing whether having this Aussie biological father could translate to dual-citizenship status and what that might mean to possible business ventures.

Even from this distance, he could hear the sighs and tears. Mom and Dad separately and together offering further explanation, the whys and the details, nobody caring to hear. Pam being the one to suggest they go for ice cream to change the tone of the evening. Jobs to get back to, the minutiae of their lives demanding attention. Over sundaes they'd likely set in concrete plans for the winter holidays, the regular Christmas kayaking trip around the San Juans in Washington State. His mother would email him about the plans. It was sure to be cold and white and snowy, she would remind him, which they all liked, in contrast to the green and red and tinsel of Christmas.

***

Dale found Rich Hand much more quickly than he could have projected, just as the middle-aged woman pulling beer in Gillagong told him he would. Jenny Kay. She'd been a looker in her day, he could tell, was from the US herself, Montana and Washington State—a point of coincidence Dale found re-markably interesting—had lived in Australia close to thirty years. Married an Aussie. Divorced an Aussie. One wall of the pub lined with framed newspaper articles she claimed to have written herself, many of them about a flood. Hard to imagine, considering the flat miles from Perth to Gillagong filled with nothing as far as Dale had seen but packed earth, roadkill kangaroo, flies, heat. Days of it. The woman offered him a beer on the house, which he took. He asked about hiring a ride. She dialed a number on the handset, asked Dale where to.

Summit Station, he said.

Summit House, she said into the phone, a giant, black, ancient thing. Heavy enough, he guessed, to stun a whale. Or a drunk Aussie.

That Hand, the woman said, as if trying to keep Dale in conversation just as he was stepping back into the roaring sunlight. He could once make a ruckus. She laughed and added, in truth, the man once *was* a ruckus. But a good person. Rich is a good person. Word did get around you were coming.

Dale paused long enough to wonder if she meant the statement as further invite, waved again, passed through the doorway and into the Gillagong street. The town's gimmick appeared to be the roughneck look. Even in this late in the twentieth century, the streets were windswept dirt, the sidewalks board plank, the storefronts weathering rough-sawn wood. But there was a touristy air about it. Prescribed. Dale tried to imagine his father—both of them—back then, at nineteen, twenty, twenty-five. *A ruckus* could mean many things, but Dale figured it meant Rich Hand had spilled blood.

The ride from Gillagong to Summit House took hours. Whether it was Dale's offer of a sandwich or general bad demeanor, the driver, who from his few spoken words sounded clearly Aussie, remained sullen throughout. Dale tried to ask questions about the rather stunning silhouettes of land formations wavering in the distance, plus other odd geographic features such as sudden gullies and drop-offs, flora, wildlife. A few nesting birds looked like they belonged on cereal boxes.

Barely hesitating long enough to drop Dale at a gate and tell him to push the button on the squawk box, the man took off in a dervish of dust and exhaust.

Most stunning were the whitewashed fences surrounding a vast, irrigated spread of land. Huge water storage tanks, run with lines of hose, sprayed moisture low to the ground in a mist just sufficient to make grass grow in a place born dry. The interior of Western Australia was like every place else on earth, Dale guessed: people tearing it up in favor of greenbacks. Summit House looked to be the Aussie equivalent of Disney World for the ultra-rich and dead asleep. The password? Exclusion.

Dale pushed the intercom button to announce himself. I believe a woman named Jenny Kay called ahead. I'm looking for a man who might be expecting me. Rich Hand. I'm Dale McMurtrey. We have family in common. I'm here from the US.

All was silent for a few minutes. He could leave. He could turn around. It must be possible to hitch a ride back to Gillagong. Might not happen until morning, still, he could sit at the road and wait.

Wait for the gate, please, a female newscaster voice said, startling him. A practiced voice. This was followed by the grate and hum of an electronic release. The gate moved laterally, the motion underscored by the faint hiss of hydraulic sound, whitewashed wood planks and black metal cross bars, the kind of fence common to bluegrass pastures and trotting thoroughbreds in central Kentucky where Russell McMurtrey kept the family racing stock.

The lane inside was graveled with igneous rock, similar to volcanic cinders, but not quite. It looked exotic, trucked in, hard to see in the dim, but Dale bet in daylight the color would make a distinct complement to the transformed Kuyunga flats in front of him. Wondering at the ease with which the gate unlatched, Dale shifted his pack to the other shoulder. He had travelled the world making up his mind. He was here, this was now, and he was doing this.

The walk to the front porches of the main house took close to half an hour. Light from the large, three-story main house shone from every window, with people in formal dining rooms on every level clearly visible. The doors were open to the night, vibrations mingling with the noise of silver tapping plates and cups landing on saucers, domes lifted and returned to serving trays. Management went all out on this set-up, Dale whispered. Men—patrons and servers—were dressed in black tails and ties, women in loose, sparkly sheaths and period gowns, hair bobbed or coiffed to match. The theme and era appeared to be 1940s European aristocracy. Dale could have been spying on a film set, so exact was the detail. *So Casablanca.* He expected Humphrey Bogart and Ingrid Bergman any minute, then became aware of the image he must be projecting standing alone in the doorway taking it all in—an American with a backpack. Must be a writer or a movie star. A very tall black man with Aboriginal nose and lips wearing white gloves walked over and waved Dale toward a parlor adjacent to the dining room. *Sil vous plait?* he said, his body language, not his voice, providing the question mark.

English, Dale said, realizing the language drifting from the tables as he walked through did sound like French. It surprised him to think wealthy Australians were as easily seduced by mirages as Americans. He also didn't think of the Outback when he thought of amusement parks. This must be something different. Maybe a reunion of people who'd worked or lived or passed through the place or just had a certain passion. Somebody's idea of theatre.

You are here to see Mr. Hand, the waiter said, now using newscaster English, congruent with the woman's voice at the gate. Again—*practiced.*

Yes, sir, Dale said, already liking this man, despite what he was stuck doing to earn a dollar, likely tossing coins in a jar to save for a life of his choosing. Probably degreed, too. Maybe Dale would do a project with the man once he made it out of this oddball place.

Mistress Jenny Kay called. She was worried—if I may quote—the spinifex might have opened and swallowed you.

Spinifex, Dale said, bile for no discernible reason welling, leaving a raw place between his heart and throat, behind his sternum.

Desert scrub. You likely noticed it. A local term for distance. Mistress Jenny Kay must have thought you capable. She's sharp that way, and you're a Yank stepping into empty spaces.

Empty spaces? He must have more US education than I have, Dale thought. Literature, no doubt. Evangel Mattox was the name on the card the man handed Dale, then pointed down a wide hallway with draped tables, gilt-framed paintings, and lit sconces. If you'd like to freshen yourself? he said, and, once again, not as a question. I'll see what Mr. Rich is up to. If you need someone to retrieve me in the meantime, tell them you need to speak to Evangel.

The urge to urinate had instantly grown out of proportion. Dale barely made it into the restroom and unbuttoned his Levis before a tank-sized ration of urine burst forth. Adrenalin. The faintly yellow guts of his day swirling around and down, gone as if they never existed. Dale washed his hands while looking in the mirror. Why had he not noticed the minute drooping of his lazy eye, the one doctors strengthened by having him wear a patch over the good one in middle school? Not noticed the faint ridge to his brow, the slow kink of his hair, the slightly flattened width of his nasal bridge, the skin that never completely lost its tinge the way the other kids' did after summer ended? His mother must have hypnotized herself into not seeing his father in him. Of course, he was saying all this having not seen Hand yet.

Back in the parlor on a tufted leather settee sat a man for whom Dale needed no introduction. The moment of first sight was the moment all conjecturing lost power. Previous questions flashed like gun powder into answers. Rich Hand was, in older terms, mulatto, a coffee-and-milk blend of the two extremes of human coloring. The fact that humans continued to think about each other according to color had always bored Dale.

We've set a table for you, Mr. McMurtrey, Evangel said.

You knew I was coming? Dale said.

Miss Birdie called to say a bloke named McMurtrey was on his way, Rich Hand said. I figured she meant the other McMurtrey. Your mom's old man. I knew him. I'd go rounds with him again. Blew me back when she said you'd be bloody young for it. Of course, him and his missus had two kids, a joey and a sheila. Figured secondly you'd be the joey grown. What was his name? But you ain't. I hear that much in your voice, mate. He'd be older. You don't sound old enough. You're a question on feet. Unless you're a solicitor, come to tell me I've a pot of gold in somebody's will. You bloody hell ain't selling Hoovers. Not to this mob.

Evangel seated them, bowed, took his leave. Dale didn't know whether to speak. Rich looked shriveled, older than sixty-nine in California might look, which is the age Dale's mother Jeanne had calculated Hand to be. She insisted she couldn't be certain, though, because she knew little about Rich, other than the obvious.

My brother's name is Marv, Dale said finally.

Too right. That it'd be, Rich said.

Well, Dale said, I'll tell my story if you want to hear it. Suddenly a story's what I've got.

Instead they talked around the subject while chipping at a meal. The lamb was easy as butter and the *sauce á la menthe* made a fine excuse for breaking with manners and sopping it with the *pain au levain*—language given to him by Evangel as he served each dish. The bread was also known as damper, Rich made known. It grew out of necessity, he said, a staple of the Aussie Outback. Rich thought Dale might have heard it called sourdough, indicating also that it was his personal specialty, and he'd bank on his damper against any Yank's. Beneath the polite conversation, Dale toyed with the odd coincidence of this meal being remarkably similar to the one he'd eaten the night of his mother's truth session.

Rich went on to talk about how his eyesight diminished as he got older, at first only the edges of a carpet bled onto wood floor planks and leaves looked like smears of green, like painted pictures. Eventually his visual field shrunk to the diameter of a face-sized pipe. Then pieces of the world started coming up missing, sucked into their backdrops such that objects at a distance had to be described to him. He was working here at Summit House and it still a sheep station by the time people started to notice and comment about him not seeing right what every other chap was seeing. Yet the boss kept him on the roster, gave him a bunk and the kitchen, caught by his cooking habits. More money in cane, but he didn't prefer it. If nobody else, Summit Station folks would know him when he died. He hadn't been a perfect man, but he ended to his hard-driven ways early enough to save his soul, earn favor with most.

Dale finally said, Jeanne McMurtrey is my mother. She says you are my father.

Rich smiled, bright and large. So you're what come of it. Little Jeanne.

Yes, Dale said, wishing to know how Rich felt, gazing at the human his lust had created.

I wondered. I was hungry for her like a blackfella for grubs. She had to have been ripe. I been around sheep. You can tell.

Rich dropped his posture as if shot. Bloody hell, he said. Oughtn't have to hear your mom talked about like that. Take my head. It's called for.

Dale held back the urge to laugh. He was near forty years old, talking to a half-Aboriginal Australian man who decades ago diddled his sweet, fresh-faced mother. Did he want the details?

Rich said, But I tell you this, she was pretty as gold and brighter than she was a vision.

Dale decided nobody was guilty. It was biology. Pure biology. If they'd been bugs on the ground, no one would have noticed. I've seen pictures, he said. I know my mother turned heads. I'd rather hear your story. Your life before and your life since.

Rich searched the air low with his hand, pulled a chair around for his feet. Evangel came by with a bottle and a set of cut-crystal tumblers. Evangel, Rich said, this chap be my blood and bone, fair dinkum. How's he look? Fair to the sheilas? Rich's smile was wide and contagious. Dale bet even age and blindness hadn't restrained the bastard.

Sir, no one could deny a resemblance when the two of you are sitting side by side, Evangel said, his smile and eye's gleam both teasing and insinuating. Made Dale wonder how many more versions of himself wandered about the Aussie desert.

He took a glass, held it steady while Evangel poured. Still have patrons, Evangel said, when Dale offered him the drink first.

What is this place, anyway? Dale asked. Why the fancy attire?

Attire, Rich said, as if tossing back a bad fish.

Politicos, Evangel said. Fundraiser.

In Australia? For the French?

No, no, no, *Monsieur*. Ze guests, zay be only speaking ze French, Evangel said, the exaggerated accent taking the place of his earlier command of the real thing. Zees ess, how you say in Ammellica, only ze play-acting? Eet ees theatre, *Monsieur*. Very soon, a meerdur she weel occur? And zee guests weel spend ze weekende trying to solve ze meerdur? *Oui, oui?*

Feigning pain, Dale said, Jesus Christ. How much a plate?

Two-hundred fifty thousand Australian dollars per couple, Evangel said, back to West Coast English.

Sheesh, Dale said, one twenty-five thousand US.

Close, Evangel said, picking up dinner plates. One bottle?

Join us and make it a party, Dale said. Damn, he liked these guys.

Tell him about your granddad, Mr. Rich, Evangel said.

I'm about to, Rich said, draining the shot, then searching with his fingers for first the bottleneck, then the glass rim, joining the two for the refill. Dale watched the action, moved by its casual accuracy, thought of the progression of blindness, wondered if when Hand felt a thing, he thought of the color. Maybe it was just the booze, the way the candle caught the facets of the cut crystal, but time froze, the camera only in his brain, nonetheless the picture taken—his mulatto father pouring scotch, the Aboriginal in tails and white gloves clearing dishes, the time-squandering American thinking himself important enough to trace the line of his pedigree. A fad. Nobody in the States thought about heritage until *Roots*.

Evangel turned his back on them, off to the kitchen with a sterling tray full of the remains of their dinner. Dale caught himself eyeing the man's ass. He hoped Rich's compensatory powers didn't extend to intuition. He didn't want to admit to sexual ambiguity. Not when Hand's virility was so obvious. Dale forced confidence into the motion of drinking and pouring the next round.

As if cued, Rich reached across and put a palm to Dale's forearm. The musculature and bone structure of the two appeared identical. Dale's skin was paler, darkly haired. Rich's arms were hairless.

Let me tell you a thing, Rich said. He stood and leaned as if to whisper, and did, indeed. *Come the dark, all cats are gray.*

Rich dropped back to his chair, laughing hard and pounding the table for accent, rattling the silver and threatening the bottle of scotch. His lips peeled back from his teeth to show black-edged mulberry gums. Rich settled down, chair legs dropped to the floor. Fingered the bottle neck and the glass lip again. My grandfather, he began, was not a black nigger from

Africa as I was let to know for most of my grown-up life. But he *was* a black man. I bet you thought I was blackfella, didn't you? Most do. I did until I got to be in my twenties.

By the time Dale left Summit House, his life story bore no resemblance to the one he'd have recited a day earlier. He kept seeing his newfound father, Rich Hand, whose induction into the world had been both incident and accident, and whose genes became a mindless gale, their need to prevail powerful enough to extinguish a mother's devotion and ability to limit her already-born children's exposure to betrayal. His mother, at her current age, was strong-willed but still vaguely naïve. What had she been on the day of his conception? Well over twenty-one, the contemporary age of adulthood, supposedly; smart but provincial. She'd have been no match for a saunter-ing Aussie. The same man—this *bloke*—awoke one sunny a.m. tired of his own shenanigans, thankful to have survived him-self, then initiated a respectable life for himself. It could be argued Dale's mother owed Rich Hand a debt of explanation for bearing his child without his knowledge. What to do now? Rich already said he didn't want life to change. He'd weath-ered enough. He had no gumption for travel to America and was clear about not wanting the others to show up at Summit House.

Then there was the other story. Jesus. Cherise Tuor. *Shit!* Out to leave her husband *and* a house full of kids? Dale wished for an early photo of Rich. Must have been a pretty devil. Dale asked Hand about the chances of him having also fathered a baby with Cherise. She was feeding, Rich said. Can't make one when you've one at the breast. It's a well-known rule of the body.

Dale told him he wasn't so sure about the accuracy of that theory. Rich got silent then, picked up his cane and strolled through the doors to the wide corridor, whistling.

Except for a few fits and tosses, Dale failed to sleep that

night, at last finding comfort just before dawn on the fainting couch, which he draped with sheets, plumped up a pillow edged in lace and covered himself with a white silk comforter. By the time he stared at himself in the shaving mirror, the world was up, busy, and full of sound. He made his way to the kitchen to look for his father, instead found Evangel, bargaining with the staff over the day's duties. Two caterers were ill, so those who were cross-trained had to step up. A bonus will be awarded you, Evangel was saying, in perfect Queen's English, to which heads nodded, apron strings were tied, people walking away energetically, and without grumbling.

He left, Mr. McMurtrey, Evangel said. He won't return until you are gone. He's studying the situation. It's his way. You'll hear from him. He's quite happy to know you are his family.

Dale felt split in the gut, embarrassed, couldn't hold back the crying. He hadn't cried since—when?

That's good, Evangel said. Tears are honest. Saying good-bye is sad.

Rather than hail the driver, Dale filled his water bottles and a pack-style bladder, asked Evangel for bread and nuts, whatever might not spoil over a day or two. He had decided to walk the many miles to Kuyunga, toward the Kimberley, to see if he could hitch a ride, because it had been part of Rich's turf. He knew he could die from the elements, but he also knew Kuyunga was only a few hours' walk. He had enough water for that. Maybe he'd run across work there, work of the kind Rich Hand might have done, become part of the scenery. His visa was good for months yet. Although he couldn't work legally, and he wasn't ready to sort through the dual citizenship possibility. Still, there was always the black side of the table. He wasn't sure what else he wanted from the journey other than bare feet on ground that held traces of Rich's younger footsteps. He'd also planned to return to Jelico, to the Outbound park, to the location of his conception, even though neither the crazy man who had spelled out his name—*P-i-o-t-r, not P-e-t-*

e-r—nor the older, shriveled Mr. Tuor had seemed capable of providing reliable information.

He didn't know what to ask them, anyway.

Hiking across the landscape of the Australian west, parched and red-earthed with the Kimberley to the northwest and mirages to the east, Dale's thinking rambled: camels, the new model Mustang, vanishing rain forests. Now and again a rattle-trap Cherokee or Range Rover or flatbed blasted by to boil and shift the dust, but none responded to his out-turned thumb. He laughed manically when he remembered the size of Uma Thurman's thumbs in *Even Cowgirls Get the Blues*. Dale realized why handkerchiefs were a predictable part of an Outback wardrobe, tying his around his throat to pull over his mouth and nose as needed, glad for the money he'd spent on a bush hat. The miles racked up. He got thirsty, hungry, then thirsty again, got worried enough about water he considered whether to save his piss, until he reached the point where even that wasn't being produced. Toward the end of the day, an hour after he'd completely run out of water, just as he was starting to think he'd better flag down the next vehicle, the outline of Kuyunga became visible. What he thought had been ten miles on the topo map must have been closer to twenty. He'd trade a kidney for a beer and the chance to unleash a list of superlatives against the environs—*flattest, hottest, dustiest, ugliest, cruelest*. He'd walked from the green of an invented world along the natural but coarse, brazen landscapes of another. What Summit House was by invention, Kuyunga appeared to be by the lack thereof. It was exactly what he'd imagined Rich's world to look like. Labor-driven, time-abraded squalor. Call it his California influence, his Hollywood brainwashing. He wanted what he knew he was going to find: hard-faced men in oiled dusters, men who drove cattle and ripped sugar cane and slaughtered sheep bare-handed. He wanted men who were silenced by rain, succored by heat, crazed by booze, unfettered by obligation, yet shattered by the fragility of their world. He knew there was other grueling business in the region, mines, etcetera, but he didn't care about them. Plus, now that it was the obvious possibility, he wanted evidence that he was built of a similar brand of grit, not the soft-muscled forearms of the man who raised him, Russell McMurtrey, who descended from mere money and politics. What did he think of his mother, a woman who risked ruin for the sake of lust? It wasn't a question. Certainly he knew what he thought of the man rawbacked enough to do the ruining: he wanted to be just like him. Who wouldn't? He also wanted to prove that being the offspring of an Aussie fuck was much more than bush hats and funny speech, as American marketing insisted. Kuyunga made it look —*fair dinkum*—like that was the exact case.

Which is to say, Kuyunga was hyperreal. Raw. Every board and face branded by heat. Heat that blackened blood as quick as skin was scraped, dragged the wings of listing chickens to every stripe of shade that wasn't occupied by a dog or human. Nothing clustered, save flies, which competed for dampness on brows, eyes, lips, nostrils, even expirations. Every day the same: will it be hotter outside or hotter inside? Will closing shades and doors mean the difference of a degree up or a degree down?

No women, as far as Dale could see, only men with backs broad as railroad tracks from cutting sugar cane. This is what Dale had decided to find out about himself—whether it was in him to survive working the cane fields. Funny. As long as he thought he was Russell McMurtrey's son, he strived to accomplish only beyond the limits of that father. Now he felt open to entirely new limits. He'd passed the tests of brain and money. Now he'd see what muscle and genetics would buy.

Dale walked toward a pub named Boswick's. None of the other handful of businesses appeared open except the fuel station—petrol station, more accurately. Certainly no dearth of autos in the vicinity. In fact, wind from passing vehicles and overhead fans was the only moving air. Children sat on the

roadsides waiting to catch the breeze, which obviously con-
founded his earlier observation, because if there were children,
there had to be women. He wondered what people did for gro-
ceries, medical care. No church. Where did people shop for
clothing?

Although clothes apparently weren't in big demand, either. Men wore pale-colored shorts of a type his *Fodor's* called
stubbies, a sleeveless undershirt (called a singlet in *Fodor's*, a
wife-beater in the US), boots, a wide-brimmed hat and a handkerchief around the neck, and that was it. Inside Boswick's,
the one woman he finally did see sat directly under one of
the slow-spinning fans writing in a notebook. She was wearing dark shorts, a white shirt, the requisite kerchief, and a hat
hung flat against her spine from a chinstrap, which appeared
as a stripe across her throat. She gestured in Dale's direction
as he came in, dark eyes slow to absorb him, saying nothing,
going back to her work. She was a bit dirty looking, but how
could she not be?

The barman was fair-skinned with grayed hair, looked as if
once he had been meatier, skin hanging from his great height
and limbs. He seemed sucked in about the middle, bent, or
toppled, faded tattoos of ravens plus a series of lightning bolts
running along his upper arms. Dale appreciated the man's
vest, which was black leather, lasted across the front with a
suede strip. The word that passed through Dale's mind upon
first seeing the guy was *fortunate*. He didn't know why, just
that it heightened his day to lay eyes on the dude.

The man's reaction to Dale was a bit different. Jesus Christ
and the Virgin Mother, the man said, his accent Scottish, not
Aussie.

Dale didn't know how to respond. He felt very American.
He was second-guessing his plan to inquire about cutting cane.
A pint, he said, finally, trying not to stare at the tattoos on the
back of a second man in the kitchen leaning over a large grill.
This one was younger, naked from the waist up, towel hanging

from his back pocket like that of every short order cook in the world, head shaved bald, a pair of peacocks filling the whole of his back beak-to-beak. He stopped mid-flip of the spatula to look at Dale, mouth open, hand-rolled cigarette hanging by its paper.

You see what I see, Jimmy D? the barman said.

I sure as fuck do, Robert, I sure as fuck do, the kitchen man said. I'm seeing myself a ghost. He looks dry as a turnip.

Up until last week, Dale was a sane and dependable guy living in a nice, upper-class mansion in California. These guys were making him feel like he had grown two blue noses. A month ago his worst worry was his long-standing ambivalence toward his sexuality. Now he was sitting on a dark plank of a stool in a hell populated by goons who looked like they could just as easily skewer him.

I see it exact, the kitchen man continued. Bloody prawn's kin of Rich Hand, he said, raising his fingers in a tough-guy gesture to pull at his cigarette, feigning to watch the smoke trail toward a wobbly fan perched by an open window. Looks like him exact. You know that about yourself, mate?

A fact, a fact, the barman—who was apparently named Robert—said, looking Dale square on. I don't doubt Rich Hand made a pup or two. Just never thought I'd bloody lay eyes on it. He's a piece back in the spinifex if you want to find him. Had an eye for the lasses, he did. Not many come through Kuyunga. Too hot too long for 'em. Got his ass in the crosshairs a time or two, he did. Bloodied him up in front of me own pub. Sold that pub to Miss Birdie, Miss Jenny Kay, I did. Now she be a shiny lot. Married that dark-haired Jelico bloke, she did, the dark-haired one, the one I always swore had to be Hand's, too. Not the twill-brained one. A sorry lot that was. Hand was after all the women. We all was, but he got 'em. We didn't. Fancy a pint did ya say, mate? Well, we ain't got nothin' but tinnies. Ah, pie hole. Shut me pie hole, will ya, Jimmy? I can't shut her up long enough to toss him a tinnie. Toss him a tinnie, will ya? I want me a good look at his face. Sorry day when ol' Rich turned blind. People get old you gotta forgive 'em. Came from Sydney, he did. Pap a sailor. Jimmy D? Weren't Hand's pap a sailor or sommat? Ah, never mind. I never use to go on. Had me the apoplexy, I did. Never used to say a thing to nobaught, now I can't keep meself shut up. Jimmy D? Toss me a tinnie, will ya? I think I might be done. Tell me boutyaself, old chap. Jimmy D! Ah, bloody hell. Have to fetch it me bloody self, I reckon.

The barman walked off without returning. The woman in the background giggled. Robert, she said. He's my pap. They call him Robert the Bruce. Or just The Bruce. He used to be big. I keep watch on him. He's had a stroke. He was messing with you. We got word you was coming. Rich called himself. You still want the grog, I'm guessing. The Bruce thinks we still only got tinnies. He forgets we got the Kelvinator. Bought it off of Summit House when it was switching them out. I can pour you a pint or toss you a tinnie.

Two. Pints, Dale said. I'll buy two so I don't have to ask again.

Bollocks, the girl said, pouring the dark liquid from the taps into two quart jars, then setting them in front of Dale.

You Hand's for sure? she asked.

Her inflection was less rural than her father's had been, and Aussie, not Scottish. As if she must have been raised in or near a city.

It appears, Dale said.

People like the old boy good enough, she said. His stories are old stories. Nobody holds the past against nobody out here. Calendar cures all, I reckon.

Last night I stayed at Summit Station. House. Summit House, Dale said. What the hell?

We still call it Summit Station. Things ain't what they used to be.

I know my father is an old man. And there are some pretty

strange people who don't mind paying a lot of money to support a political candidate.

Well, the woman said, they might raise a few dollars at a fling like that, but it'll be all. All they'll need. Here in Oz we're not like you Americans. It's about the best plan. A good plan costs nothing. Blokes don't put on fancy campaigns because they're not allowed. Plus, the very people they want to vote for them are put off by waste. Don't take money to run an election. Just a plan.

Well, don't hold me liable for America's politics, Dale said.

Bloody hell, no, the woman said. Just settin' 'em up. Didn't want your opinion taking the wrong flair, either. Pretty bold of you, hiking out here without company. It's almost forty kilometers from Summit Station and dead heat.

Tell me about it, Dale said. Look, I don't have an opinion about anything at the moment, except a bed and a meal. Happy to buy either or both if you've got them. And another beer.

***

Dale awoke the next morning face-to-face with Robert the Bruce's daughter. The smell of sex on his lower abdomen, the blight of alcohol in his throat and head. He didn't want to wake the woman, but his overwrought bladder barked. Her skin was fair as her father's. What mother had made her into the constellation of soft and tough she was? Only one night, but the relief was fathomless. He had slept with a woman and enjoyed it. Hopefully not an affront to Robert the Bruce. He did not want to end up as his bio-father had, counting and comparing the relative worth of broken ribs to the particulars of a woman.

He edged his leg off the mattress. The woman stirred. Jimmy D? she said. Dale winced. Shit. Not the kitchen man.

Nope, Dale said, before pulling shut the toilet door. Dunny, was the Aussie slang for it. A chunk of mirror hung from a rustic knot of twine over the hole in the wood floor. Years of piss stains and poorly-aimed squats colored the lid and edges of the orifice, which looked bleached and scrubbed. The image in the mirror was not a bad one, not the face of a man who had drunk too many beers to remember one entire evening of his life. He practiced the words he'd use to convince Robert the Bruce's daughter that he did not ordinarily couple with strangers, imagined her reassuring him that the slip of Jimmy D's name was a fluke, not a habit. At least he prayed that was the case. He didn't want a standoff with Jimmy D.

The woman called from the bedroom. Bloody hell, she said. On again, off again, Jimmy D and me. Mostly off of late. Old habit.

Dale walked back to the bedroom. Any place to clean up? he asked.

The woman pointed. Back of the house. Don't forgive it, then, but do you fancy a cuppa?

Dale kissed her. She was older than he thought. About the same as he. Nothing to forgive, he said. I'd be glad for coffee, if you have it. Tea if you don't.

The woman fell back on the pillow as if in relief. Morgan, she said. No, not another bloke. My name. As in Morgan's Raiders. The Bruce keeps books about the US Civil War.

The shower was rubber hose wired to a bucket with holes in it hanging from two poles and a cross-piece. No drape. The baked earth under it was already hot as asphalt. Dale could see no other buildings in any direction. Odd trees grew nearly perpendicular to the house, which was of a style he knew to be called a station house, a rectangle with a reflective metal roof and covered porch all the way around. The trees' silhouettes looked like coastal scrub disfigured by wind and blowing salt. The effect was slightly spooky. He turned the faucet, thinking to cool the ground before he stepped onto it, when Morgan showed with a wooden yard chair and a bucket and told him to figure it out. He hung his towel from a nail, one of several driven at intervals into the poles, situated himself on the chair, used the bucket for a footrest, lathered soap to rub on head and hair, arms, face, rinsed from his genitals the scent of the night before. Stupendous, vivifying, standing under a bucket full of holes in the Australian Outback after a night of beer and sex with a tavern owner's daughter. *Morgan Boswick.*

Dale started the drying process, head to feet, feeling the best he had felt in years. He wondered whether there was a future here for him. Whether this alignment with Morgan was a convergence of substance. He walked back to the porch, making mud from the dirt, the muck pushing between his toes only briefly, because it dried in an instant, crumbling to silt.

Morgan sat at the table with her hair untied, an open book and a mug of tea, stirring, contemplative. Here's a cuppa, she said. Jar coffee. Rare I keep it. Dungarees is in the corner.

Thank you, Dale said, steadied himself against the sway. He sipped the reconstituted coffee, found it not half bad, looked about, felt the woman tracking him, wondering. The living area was spare, two small zinc basins on a waxed counter where the dishes got washed and rinsed, hot plate, yellow-checkered oil cloth—the lone contrast to an environment otherwise grayed plank. Well, that wasn't fair. The window curtains had faded squiggles in various washed out-colors. A ladder made a diagonal dissect along the opposite wall broken otherwise only by a single shelf of books. Dale assumed this meant a loft, perhaps extra sleeping rooms, wondered whether the bed they'd used was normally occupied by Robert the Bruce.

Regret don't govern me, Morgan said after a while, so don't make like you skipped school. She had risen to the hotplate to grab the aluminum pot, pour hot water over more tea leaves, coffee crystals spooned from a jam pot. She laughed, touched his shoulder. I sex what I want to sex, is all. Jimmy D still don't like it, but that's his problem.

Dale wondered what LA types would do with women who dropped babies in the dirt and chewed the umbilicus 'til it broke. Women who could butcher a sheep, stitch a wound.

***

Something occurred. An occurrence. Flashes. Light. Quick light. Glint. Steel. Slice. Cut. Human limbs. Sweat. Unbathed flesh. Lunges. Lunge. Lunging. Too little sound. Until. Morgan screaming. Curses. Beautiful. Loud. Women cursing was beautiful. Dale had not known this. From a narrow distance came the laughter of men. Perspective. A pinpoint perspective. Distance. Far away. The sound of male glee. Heard the world over in response to hockey, soccer, football broadcasts. Except. No TV.

Tried to rise. Back on his seat, on his ass. Fell to his seat on his ass. His abdomen. Why was he staring at his abdomen? What was wet? What was blood? Was it squirting? Why was Morgan's voice shrill, climbing, bouncing off the rafters, echoing across the globe into outer space? Why was the day black? Why did a voice scream back with extra force, Shut up woman or I'll peel your face? Why blood? Why was blood soaking his shirt? Dripping to the board floor? *Are you kidding me? Jimmy D took a stab at me?* Robert the Bruce at the door with cans of beer. *Tinnies.* Jimmy D dancing like a jester, waving a thin-bladed knife, overturning tables, lunging and plunging the blade, feigning another stick, laughing and working up courage for a second impale.

Give us a break, asshole! Morgan cried out, dashing the knife from Jimmy D's hand with a tossed book. Get out of my house. Both of you.

He scissored your own mam, Hand did, Robert said.

It's a lie and a rumor, Morgan said. Mam made me swear never to believe it. She didn't do it. Besides, this is not the same man. This is not Rich Hand.

***

The mash of tires against grit beside his ear deafened him. *Here* was not Morgan's plank floor but the hot dusty ground. She was driving away with Jimmy D and Robert the Bruce. His beauty. Leaving Dale twisted on his side such that he could not see it yet could feel his hat on his head. Water bottles cold between his knees and feet. Was that his pack beneath his head? Smell of rusty blood. His lower back naked against the round of a dead tree trunk. Leafless branches making shade in strips. The flies a black writhing mass above and around him. Tried the Aussie salute, but no good. Around him all was silver mirage, floating vertical waves of heat.

MERL CHATCOLET

MERL HATED PICKING UP Americans who died in the bush. Always had empty water bottles. You could tell a Yank by the outfitter-type water bottles. Aussies would have an empty sixer. Yanks had pretty bottles, backpacks, and good footgear, but never a tarp for shade or salt tabs. Always full of gorp and granola bars, black with flies, mumbling about throwing stones at vultures. The worst already had their bones picked. Some were a trail of pieces.

He was feeling guilty about spatting with his wife at such a bloody sorry time as the occasion of her mom's death. He pissed her off by saying sure as the sun rolls he'd be the one to drag home her newfound American half-brother. He's a Yank. He's in the desert, Merl said. History is its own testimony.

This occurred right after she told him the story she heard at the diner in Sydney. All spats aside, in one flash of an eye this new information changed and relieved his wife. To finally know what it was that drove her mother off. Passion. With all her magazines and movies, Lesa could accept passion as an excuse. At some point he'd also be the one to tell it to Miss Jenny Kay over at the Tanzey-Davis in Gillagong, who would have an interest since she once had been married to Lesa's brother Martin, who was rumored to be striving toward being an American citizen himself. Obviously a way would have to be worked out for the two blokes to get to know each other.

Now here Merl was with a call from Kuyunga. The farthest end of his jurisdiction and a trip he dreaded. Kuyunga folks were as scary as some of the ones depicted in motion pictures made up about the Aussie Outback. Even the blackfellas didn't like to go near 'em. Despite being armed, he doubted himself to be a match if one of those Kuyunga madmen wanted to make a sport of him. He didn't like having to camp out in the bush. People out that direction had been found shot from way off. High-powered rifle rounds of the type normally used for shooting feral pigs. Generally, it was reckoned in the district to take Australia's military intelligence to ferret out the perpetrators. Proof positive of what isolation did to people's civility.

Gladly, this Dale McMurtrey was not any place close to dead. They'd stuck him with what looked to be a narrow blade in the region of the spleen, and had the good graces to call it in so to avoid an international murder case. Dropped outside Summit Station. Feeble and sunburned, otherwise upright and waving when Merl drove up. Looked like he'd been smart enough to shore himself with strips of shirt and a compress of eucalyptus leaves.

ANNALESA TUOR CHATCOLET

THE LETTER CAME IN 1992. Annalesa was watering the rose garden which had become her purpose and solace since her mom passed, blushes and butter yellows and reds so dark as to be black around the petal lips. Perfume lifted off them in the early hours of Jelico summer, a scent distilled by the cool of the night before.

Pops had come tottering out with their morning drink of tea for her, coffee for him—a habit he'd changed to after Mom left all those years ago. Fancy a cuppa? he had said, moving the cornflower-patterned cup and saucer pair, a favorite of her mother's, toward her, his faint tremble causing a sound like shell chimes in a breeze. She had reached for it quickly so Pops would not have time to feel embarrassed. Bollocks, he said, bloody hell.

Ah, Pops, she said, too right, it's breezy, is all. Annalesa tossed one of the two sugar cubes he'd included on her saucer into her mouth and held it between her teeth, forming her lips in and out like a fish's. She spoke around the sugar, saying, kiss me, Pops. Kiss me sweet, until he put a cube in his own teeth, trying to speak similarly, the two laughing to the point they had to put down their cups, sloshing liquid onto their saucers and dissolving the other sugar cubes. She'll be right Pops, Annalesa said.

Aye. She'll be right, Pops said, pulling the envelope from his pocket and passing it to Annalesa. Is it from Marty? he asked. I think it is. Bloody hell. Bloody hell, I think it is.

Annalesa snatched the envelope from his hands, too hastily, she knew, because he recoiled. The envelope had an American stamp on it, rarely seen in their household. Occasionally an American renting out a caravan received his mail at the Outbound box. This one had been a flag wavering, or appearing to waver, the way it was drawn with its middle offset. All this time, very few notes. Once or twice a call. Always asked the same things. Any word from Jenny Kay? Piotr still writing letters to the Prime Minister? Otherwise nothing since the last when she told him Jenny Kay finally had divorced him for desertion, charges of abandonment, which didn't require his signature, the papers waiting for him in the family lockbox at First Commonwealth Bank in Denton. Never once did he inquire about Annalesa's life, about Merl, about Mom. Not that Annalesa didn't try ringing him up after Mom's death, but where would she bloody ring to? Admittedly, she didn't try as hard as some might.

What's he saying? her father asked. The two of them had dropped onto deck chairs, passing the envelope back and forth, taking turns examining the paper of it, Pops tracing the edges with his shivery hands. Crikey, he said, and started to cry. You don't think he's dead or sommat?

Annalesa had commenced tears, too. Dead blokes don't write letters, Pops, she said. She felt her family's hurtful existence pasted inside that envelope. *The envelope please* the chap said on the telly whenever the notable prize was about to be awarded. Here she was on a deck chair at the Outbound, nothing to say for her life but that she married a good bloke and appreciated the morning smell of roses. Sure as shit the envelope contained no prize. Marty certainly no prize of a brother.

Her dad's tears declined into sobs. Dead blokes don't write letters, Pops, she said again.

Oh, aye, he said, took in a lungful of air as if the first rattling breath of a newborn lamb, then laughed. They both laughed, a contagious giggle, feeding off each other to the point of wiping their eyes with their shirttails. Annalesa caught the hiccoughs. Pops went into the house for handkerchiefs to blow their noses, came back with a glass of water and a letter opener. She slipped the metal spike under the envelope flap and slit the top. It was five pages, front and back, coil-bound paper, his script just as Annalesa remembered it: flattened and creaky in places, loopy and elongated in others. Marty had the most inconsistent penmanship of any she'd ever seen, and she was prone to notice such things. If she had one interest she'd like to develop further that was it: penmanship analysis and what it revealed about a person. She admired her husband Merl's discreet, confident, blocky style. It was one of the first things she noticed. He wrote like a copper ought to. Like he knew how to take charge.

Well, Pops, she said, do I read it quiet or read it aloud to the both of us?

Reckon to the both of us. Says Tuor on the front. I'm Tuor and you're Tuor. Tuor then Chatcolet. But I reckon Marty doesn't know that much, does he?

Annalesa sighed. Marty knows, Pops. We got married before he was gone. You recall the bloody wedding, surely.

I bloody hell reckon, her father said.

Annalesa wished one of those game show blokes had been around to ask her the question: *And what, Mrs. Chatcolet, would you guess to be the contents of this letter?* Because she felt she had known what it was going to say without reading a line. She bloody knew Marty was going to sound like Piotr. The first page started without so much as, Sis, how's the world? Rather with mercury climbing the cold tile walls of his shower stall at his flat in Perth right before he split from Jenny Kay. Then tales of cowboys, a US FBI conspiracy, cracked mountain men. He claimed to have even tried university, except she knew the US didn't give free education to foreigners. Even Americans paid for their own.

Next he chattered about going for citizenship, how hard he bloody well had to study for the examination, which showed him how capable he was, which brought him to why he decided to write her. Did Annalesa have his old Peabody School books? He wanted his geography and a history book. The US Department of Immigration study guide information didn't match what he'd remembered from being a kid. He was dead certain he remembered different stories, plus, even though he had his naturalization records signed and secure, he still wanted to make the comparison so he could bring it to official attention. Oh, and did Annalesa have his original birth papers? He'd gotten official copies, had to for the Yanks, still he wanted the original proof. He wanted to frame it. Did Annalesa reckon to scurry about looking for ancient manuscripts?

Then, *Ha*. Martin had written this bit of laughter inside a little comic book bubble, a circle with a teat at the edge of the page. Ha. Ha. Annalesa found the caption humorless. She looked at Pops, who wasn't laughing either.

Write back, Pops had said, putting his large-veined but bony hands on his knees, then standing and pulling himself to height in a way she hadn't seen since he used to have to make decisions about Piotr. Against the backdrop of his sun-worn face and milk-white hair, his eyes appeared blue and pungent as a November sky, alight with chill and fire. Tell him to get his ass the bollocks home and retrieve his own shit. Tell him to see if he can do it without shuffling dirt on his mom's foot beats.

Annalesa heard the creaking, depleted sound in her Pop's angry voice, which formed a resolve in her chest solid as a steel spike. She would not contribute to a measure meant to keep Marty parked on the opposite pole of the globe. The rumpled and decaying pieces of her family's kinship had to be straightened so her father could have his peace before he passed on from this world, too. So, yes, she would pen a letter back, contents her choosing, bargaining this: Martin would get his birth declaration—the books long gone—but only if he journeyed back to Drury Road to kiss the cheek of their poor dad before he was too senile to remember him.

Annalesa took her husband Merl Chatcolet along when she flew to Sydney for Cherise's funeral. Even though Merl was a bumbler when it came to feelings, neither was he a bloody dope when she couldn't do anything but bawl.

Mom's flat was slick as needles, so it wasn't the chores that galled Annalesa. It was that Mom appeared to have gotten rigid. When she compared it against her childhood, it was odd to step into a scene created by her mother that didn't feature piles of trinkets and extras. Seven sets of jeans, three of underlets. Five nurse frocks. One black travel dress. Half-a-dozen sleeveless tops. One set of white oxfords. A second pair that had never been worn. A set of patent leathers. Rubbers. One rain topper. None of the thin, flowery shirtwaists Mom had always worn before and none of the hand-pieced rugs she'd kept on the beds at the Outbound. Cherise had an old roo pelt with its pointy red-fur tail streaming off the end of the cot against plain white bedclothes. An extra set of starched cotton sheets sat folded on a shelf in the robe, waiting to be traded for the ones in current use, to be hard-cornered and tucked.

In the kitchen were one of each—a kettle, a quart pot, a crock, a salad dish, a flipper, a slot-spoon, an ironing board that fell from the wall, an automatic presser to go with it. As for dishes, there was a bit more, a relief because it meant maybe her mother had friends around for tea: six plates, six bowls, six cups, six case knives, six teaspoons in a flower-handled pattern. Six tumblers. A few serving dishes. Plus—and Annalesa and Merl pondered this—a folded cascade of dozens of white table napkins, the only thing in abundance.

What is it? Merl asked of the stack of hemmed squares. Bloody curious, if you ask me.

Merl, Annalesa said, a stack of nappies doesn't mean Mom had gone daft. Maybe she meant them for a white elephant or to donate for a cause. You can't tell.

Never said it did. Merl clicked his tongue, which she'd learned was his habit when he wanted to hold words not good to anyone. What Annalesa felt like saying but didn't, was that her mother's flat and its profound orderliness disturbed her more than the napkins.

Nurses from the hospital came to pay regards to Cherise. A few talked to her in whispers. Some of us thought your mom had gone off a bit; I just think she was homesick for her kids is all, one said when Annalesa asked about the stack of napkins. Hard to imagine those poised, prim women—including her mom—pouring out gummy bedpans. As the case was, her mother had been doing since she'd walked off down the Drury Road. Annalesa wondered if the end was truly an accident, stepping off the curb the way she did, drubbed by a boatful of water from a passing ute, most likely blinded by it. *Sydney in a monsoon could rack the rain, fair dinkum*, Merl said when she brought it up. The hospital had taken Cherise's body to the morgue, had the prefect look at it, determined there was an amount of drink in her. The bloke who signed the report liked as not Cherise was blurry from grog and got tripped up by road spray.

Gerrymandering the Fates, taking grog, we all know that. Even the merest pint or two for some of us, the prefect said, his crisp, blue uniform in contrast to the sheet-draped bodies around him. Nothing about your Mom's state to prove she took her grog by the pail. Put that with a dollar and you'll have a dollar.

Annalesa thought the prefect a prawn. What the bloody hell did that mean, she asked Merl, as they descended the steps to wait under the morgue's canopy for a cab.

Merl insisted the man was just a paid official doing his job. Grief doesn't give you right to downgrade the other bloke, Lesa, he said.

He just as well called Mom a souse, Merl. Tell me you're not defending him. Because he's a copper? Annalesa pulled her mother's raincoat around her, turned and stepped fast as she could opposite the direction Merl was headed.

Annalesa. Wait a bloody minute, she heard as she turned the corner. *Bloody drongo*. She walked quick as her breath allowed, pushing against the tightness in her chest to make herself go a little beyond that limitation, walking for what seemed like hours, past the famous Opera House, the layers of its strange architecture nestled like eggcups, glittery offices, shops. She guessed she couldn't blame Mom for busting out of the Outbound. She'd leave, too, if she didn't love so much her belly and breasts against Merl Chatcolet's back in the bed at night.

Annalesa made her way around to her mother's neighborhood. No idea of the time, so she stepped inside an open diner to ask the hour and get directions to the hospital where her mom had worked, bloody puzzle as it still was. She'd barely put her bum on the stool before the counter clerk set the cup, poured tea, passed the cubes and Carnation, then said, Saints be. The woman had black hair but no eyebrows other than what were penciled in.

I oughtn't to sit? Annalesa asked.

Yes. Crikey. Sweets, I've seen a ghost. I've seen your picture. I know exactly who you are. My very dear friend was your mother, Cherise Tuor. How did you know to come here?

Annalesa stared at the woman's face, feeling what it must have been like for her mother, seeing those eyes, nose, and mouth often enough for them to be familiar. Really? Didn't see you at the wake. Didn't, come here on purpose, neither, Annalesa said. Pure circumstance.

Well, I imagine Cherise herself had a hand in guiding you. I believe that. People get to take care of business before they move on. She wanted her children to know how much she loved and missed them. As for the wake, I never look at dead folks, the woman said. But Cherise and I knew that about each other. We always said, Don't come to mine and I won't yours. One night we drank enough to prick fingers and join blood. She was a sister. We looked out for each other. It was a shock and a loss to quite a few. I guess you must be feeling it more than anybody.

She walked behind the counter flicking switches and pulling cords from power points, pulled a flask from under the counter and dosed Annalesa's tea, lifted another teacup and poured some for herself, then the plop and clink of ice, pour of soda, squeeze of lemon. I'm Ruby. Drink what you got, she said, tossing back the fluid, turning to make more.

Annalesa noticed the angle of her torso, the chintz apron, two cups on the counter, red-rimmed, the white crazed from age. Ruby leaned forward as if to lord over something, hands to elbows on the counter. I hope you had tears for your mom's passing, she said. It was due her.

No, Annalesa started but then choked. Yes.

Good, Ruby said. Cry troughs.

Ruby sipped her drink, leaving a frosty lip impression on the red rim. Annalesa thought the woman close to Mom's age, realized her hair was the kind of black you buy from a box — the strands of a single hue but not reflecting light, rather muted. Not quite dull, but muted.

Well, she didn't know what the bloody hell to tell you, so I told her what I'd say if it were me. Worse, there's things she asked me to tell you that she and I both wished nobody needed to know, Ruby said.

Shit, Annalesa said, feeling her eye sockets shrink. Her eyes always grew swollen and tight whenever she encountered a sadness. For example, when the milk goat died. She'd cried a boatload this last week. A backward tilt of the head eased the pressure off her eyeballs, an odd and graceless pour of tea and whiskey into the cavity between her lips. Soon as the cup was empty she began making similar work of the cola version Ruby had mixed for her. Ruby appeared to take no notice of the strange action, like she knew it was normal for a dead mom's daughter to go off balance.

It's ugly news in some circles, Ruby said, human nature in others. Treat yourself to a nice vacation while you're in Sydney, because your life is apt to reshape. Find your brother who left for America and tell him. The other Yankee bloke needs to be told, too, I reckon, although it should be up to his own mom. Ruby looked at the countertop for a pause. You see her flat? Her cubby?

Annalesa now felt she had ten bloated eyeballs, none of which would focus. Ruby said something that had jarred her. What was it? Annalesa felt the dimness in her gut from shock. I don't know about a cubby, she answered. The super said nothing about a cubby.

He's a highwayman, Ruby said. If Cherise weren't due on the rent, he wouldn'ta called you at all. He's hoping for loot. You only have to look in your mom's place to know it wasn't where she kept her valuables. She gave me a print copy of her will and testament, everything parted out—what bit she had in savings and a few sentimental articles. She's got a choker and ear bobs from way back and a pearl revolver worth a fortune in a bank box. They don't pay nurses. But your mom did save what she could and wrote a little story about where each of her things came from. Your mom's family was Swiss royal, you know. Somebody way back was a prince or king. She only stayed in-country on account of your Pops. She'd have gone back to Switzerland to finish uni were it not for him.

The sounds of the diner clicked. Ice, dish machines, dessert carousel. A girl jiggled and pushed the door but Ruby waved her on. The girl nodded like she was used to it, Ruby closing before closing time.

Swiss royal. Every bloke and his mob is Swiss royal. Who's the Yank? Martin is in America, but nobody else. Don't be sharing my whereabouts with no bloke who claims to be Swiss Royal. He'll be one of those death notice trackers waiting to rob the station while the family circles the coffin. Annalesa twirled her wedding band. Wait until Merl gets this earful. Swiss royal. He'll tell me I'm a princess, all right.

Good onya, Sweets, Ruby said, reaching out a hand to Annalesa's forearm. Look, I'll say it outright. The American bloke is your brother Martin's half-brother.

Blab. Go on, Annalesa said, standing to leave. Pops used his charm before he met Mom is all. Shot it off on some town trip, so Mom never told. Don't you mean *my* half-brother, as well?

Ruby didn't say a word, shook her head, eyes drilling dead into Annalesa's. The expression on Ruby's face was dour, though not in the way of one mourning a best friend's passing. Rather one of sad acquiescence, knowing Annalesa would not be absolved of the dirty work.

About the time Ruby dropped her eyes to pick up her drink again, Annalesa felt the puzzle pieces begin to fall into place. Oh, she said, in her smallest voice, barely audible, I reckon all of a sudden I got it.

PART IV

VAL CORSICA

SHE KEYED OPEN the bottom drawer of her desk and pulled out a brass pipe, a one-hitter the size and shape of a cigarette, packed it with what was left of her emergency stash, flicked the lighter, drew the smoke deep. What an awful week. Ferris Standiford killed a Lewiston police officer. A police officer! That did not bode well for the Independent Living Center. The general consensus, according to letters to the editor in *The Lewiston Morning Tribune*, was that Ferris' best future featured him being dropped from a crop duster over Hells Canyon. The murder had inspired many of *The Tribune's* readers to dust off their typewriters and keyboards. No surprise if beer sales went up last week. Any local activity always generated an uptick in alcohol violations according to her district attorney friend, Matthew Seamus. Cheap beer was good fuel for letter writing.

Good God, Ferris Standiford. Val knew the minute she saw him he was going to joke his way to a lethal injection. Ferris was bright. Unfortunately, his was an intelligence jumbled with the inability to interpret and apply experience—every day was a new day for him—a personality deformed by abject insecurity. Not insecurity across the short span of a lapse of knowledge or understanding, as normal people experience. Instead, so fully outlandish, he was incapable of accepting that he lived in a shared world, that others occasionally had a right to command a share of the attention. He shirked intimacy via incessant jokes and histrionics. Ridiculous humor was his drug, a means of not attending to whatever was in his immediate surroundings, his mode of disconnecting. Val had long thought criminally insane people's primary compendium to be jealousy. She thought those folks were jealous as hell over not being handy at functional living. Jealousy festered in Ferris until he decided with his short stature and sparse hair to spray a lethal dose of pepper spray into that Lewiston cop. Sat on the chest of that good-looking young officer and emptied the can directly into his nose and mouth. Half-dozen pool players trailed outside and leaned on their cue sticks, watching. If it had happened inside, all of them would have been sick. As it was, only Ferris had to be hospitalized and strapped to an oxygen mask. At taxpayer expense, a point made by more than one of those letters to the editor.

Nobody knew what set him off. He'd been playing pool, laughing; the officer walked in, said howdy-do, sat on a stool, put down a dollar tip for his free cup of coffee. Before anybody registered what was happening, Ferris broke his cue in half, rammed it between the Velcro straps of Paul Crapo's bullet-proof vest and into his chest cavity, shoved him out the door onto the ground, piercing his lung, then de-holstered the man's pepper spray can and emptied it. Questions around the region were worded the same: why was that bartender so slow to call it in? Why didn't the other pool players intervene? In this day of cell phones? Doubtful Crapo would have lived even if they'd moved quicker, Val heard. The legal community was guessing those young men had bought themselves accessory raps, but hard to prove Ferris's actions were pre-meditated. The cop was pretty new. Too new for much in the way of grudges unless Ferris knew him before. Talk in her circle predicted a rash of jail suicides and aneurysms.

What *she* couldn't figure out about her part in it was why she didn't work harder to prevent Ferris from being released into ILC's custody, why she didn't follow her instincts and transfer his file back over to Hospital North. Matthew Seamus, the assistant district attorney, approached her back in January of '01, before Ferris was released from Boise the first time, at which point she told him Ferris was too big a case for Independent Living, that she hadn't the resources to monitor him closely—meaning she didn't have enough nursing staff to take on case management and home visits for Haldol injections—

nor did she herself have the expertise to deal with the criminally weird. Her specialty was run-of-the-mill-off-kilter, not *Silence of the Lambs.*

But he's not criminal, Matthew had said, which was true, at that time. Ferris' stats then featured merely a few burglaries, mental health holds, a warrant for failing to appear on vagrancy charges. Those mental health holds came about— of course—because he put himself on the bad side of ER assessments by subjecting staff to random displays of bouncy, maniacal, court-jester behaviors. Using drama and humor, in other words, to camouflage rebellion and failure to cooperate. Val guessed if that young cop, Paul Crapo, had run into Ferris in any other situation, likely he'd have laughed at the jokes, would have seen Ferris as weird but charming.

Ferris Standiford's relationship with the state of Idaho dated to the late '60s when he had been a student at the University of Idaho requiring admission to the Fifth Floor of St. Joseph's in Lewiston for the first time, because he was hallucinating, the result of a beer/LSD binge. As predicted, his hallucinations disappeared after a week in detox. Thus began decades of interaction with Idaho Mental Health Services. Homelessness. Alcoholism. Petty crimes. At no point, however, as far as the state was concerned, did his symptoms match a diagnosis. He wasn't a mental or a felon. He was just a guy who couldn't keep his shit together.

Shortly after his fiftieth birthday, he started trying to starve himself to death, which was considered a form of violence in Idaho, and which got him admitted for a long-haul stay at the state hospital in Boise. Hospital North in Orofino didn't have a psychiatrist experienced in eating disorders, so they couldn't qualify for support payments from the state. Ferris got trundled down to live with hard-core schizophrenics, instead. The kind who shuffled around talking about skyscrapers facilitating communication with aliens. The kind with torticollis from the drugs required to keep them from killing staff and fellow residents.

Fortunately, evaluation tools had become more sophisticated in recent years, so that according to latest record, Ferris had proved himself loud and clear to be randomly subject to disorganized thought and emotion, likely capable of severe violence. What he'd been doing all those years was self-medicating with alcohol, the jokes cushioning himself from his own evil potential. She'd read quite a bit about histrionics lately. It was a chemical solution to a congenital problem. The jokes and laughter produced endorphins. Ferris was like the werewolf who chains himself in his basement before a full moon—humor restrained him.

Prior to his stay in Boise, Ferris spent some time sleeping under a bridge abutment in Coeur d'Alene, living off Sterno, having enlightened conversations with Jesus Christ. Religious iconography was a fast-trip ticket to a paranoid schizophrenia diagnosis, which at last qualified him for a Haldol prescription. Once he was officially released from Boise, monitoring and oversight went to ILC—even if against Val's better judgment.

What it came down to was that Val's office was severely understaffed. She'd admitted Ferris, helped him get set up in living quarters and a part-time job, and now a he'd killed a cop. In between, according to the file on her desk, he'd been lost to follow-up after missing a number of appointments for his Haldol injections.

Lost to follow-up.

Matthew Seamus and Dan Weeks, the latter the director at Hospital North, were in her office the day after it happened.

Shame on us, Matthew said. Shame on all of us. Paul Crapo hadn't been a cop long enough to get his trouser length adjusted. Shame on you, Val. How the hell did your office lose track of him? What the fuck, Val?

What the fuck? What the fuck me? Why me? I told you. I told all of you. I've got one fucking nurse. One. One fucking person who can give insulin and B12 and all the other freaking meds these people take. I told you I didn't have the staff to handle it. She's got sixty-two on her case load. Sixty-two. As it is she's stopped doing home visits, and we've hired minimum-wage transport people to bring clients here to the office to see her instead. That's not the way it's supposed to work. We could lose our Medicaid payments. It's not legal. You wouldn't believe the juggling we do. You are not blaming this on me. You are not. I fucking won't have it.

Listen, Dan said, his reddish hair and suit looking not-fresh, as if he'd been up all night, as likely he had. We do a lot of good, Val, but there's a rotten bottom to anything, you know that. Maybe it was Crapo's time to go is all.

Weeks, Matthew said, spare us. Look. We have to make a statement. About why Ferris was lost to follow-up, Val. You're his checkpoint. You're supposed to report failure to comply.

That was it. The postmortem, so to speak, on Ferris Standiford. Val heard the front door bell's little jingle-hop, meaning her staff was back from lunch. She spritzed perfume, stepped into the bathroom, closed the door, sat down on the closed toilet. Shit. Getting high at work. It wasn't all that common. She only did it now and then. Who cared, really? So her coping was a tad off-kilter. At least she wasn't reading *Celestine Prophecy* or whatever the hell Dan Weeks was into. A PhD in philosophy and an MD with eighteen years of psychiatric practice, and he'd started reading self-help books and going to church. At least marijuana was only a little drug. Religion and self-help were such big ones. Not to mention harder to quit.

Except that the staff wasn't back at all. She didn't know what she'd heard, but it wasn't the door because the front office was empty and the coffee pot cold. Her administrative assistant, Melinda, always put it on the second she came back. High-fat lunches put everybody to sleep, so Melinda was charged with keeping the office fueled for the afternoon. Val locked her office. Drafted a note that read, *Out for the p.m. Meeting — Kamiah with potential client's family. To home after. Have my cell. Also took file on new pt. Martin Tuor. Val.*

She taped the page to Melinda's computer, put on her sunglasses, and was about to pull her keys from her jacket pocket when the door opened, the bell jingled, and Melinda herself stepped through. A curvy woman in her mid-fifties, of average height, her nylons had a run and a heel was off her shoe. Melinda shook a set of keys at Val.

These were in the door, Melinda said. I just came up on Vergil Watters. He might have been opening the door. I must have left them in the lock. I came back because I left the mail I meant to drop off. Quarterlies had to go today.

Melinda leaned over a chair, supporting herself with one arm, staying her chest with the other, as if a well-placed hand could calm her breathing. Didn't know you were still here, she said. I worried he might be going for the med closet. Do you think Vergil would do that?

Val poured a cup of water from the blue bottle spiked upside down into a machine in the corner. *Idaho Ice.* Here, she said, drink this. I'll get the Band-Aid. Do you want to go home to change? Or I might have shoes in my office that will fit.

Nah, Melinda said, I'll break the other one off or I'll glue it or go barefoot this afternoon. I have some ballet flats in my locker, I think. When we don't have appointments I wear them. I'm fine. Just winded. It scared me. Vergil took off. Do you want me to call the cops?

Val considered the scene. He wasn't a client, technically. Just a frequenter. Meaning he was allowed to hang out at the rec room, but ILC took no responsibility for him. He cleaned apartments. No SSI. He was at ILC's offices that noon out of habit. Saw the keys in the door and what? Planned to break in? Take the keys? Was he trying to do a service? Save somebody else from committing the crime? Had he meant to return the keys? Was he really after drugs?

Val couldn't decide. She put it to Melinda. What think ye?

My horoscope said two stars today. I had a flat. Didn't get to eat. I just ran a block on an empty stomach, Melinda said.

And you caught him? You caught up with him? Melinda, Vergil isn't an old man. That's impressive! Val said.

Melinda laughed. He tripped, she said. He didn't try to run. He tripped over the curb the minute he saw me running up and dropped the keys. I helped him get up, and he handed them over. I didn't even have to ask.

What did he say? Val asked.

Said he was worried about somebody else taking them. Thought he'd wait at the rec room and bring them to us after lunch. He said please don't call the police.

Shit, Val said.

I know it, Melinda said. I don't know what to recommend.

Val sat in Melinda's desk chair for a minute. You know, she said, I have a meeting in Kamiah, and I don't feel so hot. I was going to go home to lie down as soon as I'm done. We have a new intake. Another Haldol client, God help, but he qualifies to receive injections at the Health District, since he's also medical. Martin Tuor. I think I'm going to stick to my plan. Let it slide for the moment. That is my executive decision. Set up an appointment for him for tomorrow. I'll talk to Vergil and then Matthew *about* Vergil when I see them each. Enough for this week, don't you think? Oh, and I've got the paperwork on Tuor. Figured to work on it tonight from the vantage of my sofa.

I hope you're right, Melinda said.

Do you sense something different? Val asked.

No. Except Vergil Watters walks a thin line, I think. He has to work at not doing things according to old bad habits.

***

You're out of your mind, she said. They were in Dan Weeks's office in Hospital North at Orofino. Martin Tuor had taken a turn for the worse, had gone off his Dilantin, stopped showing up at the Health District offices for his Haldol injections, suffered another seizure, and had been thwarted in a suicide attempt. It was a year of money down the tubes. Plus, there was this issue of a previously-unknown—even to Martin—half-brother showing up at ILC wanting contact with him, which everyone agreed should not be allowed. What a hot-looking honey *he* was, Melinda and Val agreed. They both had always been a bit gaga over Martin, but now that they'd met his half-brother, they had a hard time reconciling which one was sexier. Break-time jokes. Eyes and Levis, Melinda said after Martin had begun stopping in for visits. All the women at ILC—clients and staff—were a bit star-struck over his muscled carpenter's build and dark good looks, not to mention the faintly exotic air his Australian parlance lent him and the fact that he was just boyish enough to activate everyone's mothering instincts.

The half-brother was named Dale McMurtrey. Melinda entered his name and contact information into Martin's chart, even though Val told him straight out that Martin was just too fragile at this time. After what happened with Ferris Standiford, a skittish Dan Weeks wanted to admit Martin to Hospital North now. If he had beds, Dan said, he'd admit everyone who was receiving Haldol injections in the community. Val concurred with Mitch Fitzgerald, director of psychiatry at St. Joseph's Regional Hospital in Lewiston, however, in thinking a month in Hospital North would alienate Martin. Both agreed recovery was dependent on his learning to fend for himself, to take care of himself physically and emotionally. To do that he must relearn trust for himself, which he could do by learning to trust ILC staff. Hospital North was definitely too strong a placement. What Martin Tuor required was a soft bed, a gentle voice, and a shoulder to lean on while his meds reached therapeutic blood levels again. He was no danger. Val was just as certain of this as she was hard set on following her instincts.

Mitch Fitzgerald was a tall, loose-limbed man with drooping eyes and unquestionable authority. He held a doctorate, had done a stint in Vietnam and ten years as the lead psychologist in an army experiment: under the Sonora Desert, a fully-contained, climate-controlled facility that was not a prison exactly, but a place where death-row felons over the age of fifty could choose to go, so long as they understood they were to be well-treated guinea pigs, the placement to be a life sentence. None of them would ever see the outside again. The outpost was such a well-guarded secret that not even the US president knew its location. That was the Cold War, however, and the Cold War was over, the recruited inmates all dead of age, interestingly enough, not disease. Mitch wouldn't reveal much more than that, in fact only talked about the place once at the waning end of a New Year's Eve party at Val's house, only Dan and Matthew and Val left to hear it, all pretty intoxicated. Made her shiver to think about it, wondering what contamination remained under the Sonoran Desert. She asked Mitch about it as he poured cups of coffee early in those New Year's morning hours.

Waited until the last inmate died, Mitch said. He was fifty in a one-hundred-year-old body. They all were. Filled the place with cement by the truckload, he said. A thousand of them. Maybe two. Day after day. Funneling into tubes in the roof. Sawed the tubes off at the ground. Hauled in top dirt, scattered every matter of desert seed, turned on the sprinklers. Once the seed took hold they cut off the sprinkler heads, too. You couldn't find it now in a million years. If they ever do, it won't be until it's a fossilized bed of human goofs. Sounds like a movie plot, doesn't it? It's truth. There's plenty our government is involved in we'll never know about. All governments. You can't spread this, Val. Shouldn't have discussed it. Booze.

Dan and Mitch argued over Martin Tuor and where the next thirty days of his life should be spent. In the end Dan passed Val a paper to sign. As executive director of ILC, Val was given power of attorney over clients. Only she had the right to pass Mr. Tuor back over to either of these men unless he got himself in the position to be forced into commitment. The form bore the state of Idaho's Great Seal. In the line marked *Placement Facility* were the typed words—ILC via St. Joseph's. Dan had come around. Martin would be checking into the Fifth Floor for rest and medication monitoring. Val shook her head in the affirmative, and smiled.

This is the appropriate placement, she said, her signature looped in a form Melinda called paw prints, as in, *Val, would you put your paw print on this?*

Agreed, Mitch said, signing his name as a series of connected streaks.

Withheld, Dan said.

Withheld? Val said. What is that supposed to mean?

It means I don't think it's a responsible decision, in light of the Ferris Standiford event. I'm going along because it's not my ass on the line. It's yours and Mitch's.

Christ, Dan, she said. What is into you? He's not one of your DMSR-IV babies. He'd discontinue his meds, left to his own. He has non-epileptic seizures. Most likely PTSD, but that's not a diagnosis. You couldn't get reimbursement until he's got his citizenship papers. It's gratis for all concerned.

Well, then why don't we just ship him back to Australia? Remember, this is very similar to the conversation we had about Ferris Standiford, minus the citizenship piece—now didn't we? Dan leaned back, hands behind his head, elbows out. We were *all* fucking worried about getting reimbursement. Life is all about reimbursement. Well, it turns out death is all about reimbursement, too. I'm just trying to save the poor taxpayers another lawsuit. Because Paul Crapo's family will sue. Mark this day on the calendar. You're going to owe me dinner, Val.

Fuck you, Dan, Val said.

Mitch, who'd been quiet throughout, leaned elbows to knees, then stood, face tight and stony. I don't think this is relevant to Martin's case, he said. He is absolutely not a Ferris Standiford. He has non-epileptic seizures. We're only assuming they are hallucinations. The Haldol is a complete experiment. Val, I'll get him transferred from med-surg to the Fifth Floor. You come by this afternoon so we can define the terms of treatment. This man does not belong in our system. He needs a boost and support, that's it. What he really needs is to go back home.

***

Val became concerned enough about her part in the Ferris Standiford lapse that she decided to nip her little marijuana habit by simply not buying any more from her vendor hero up in Coeur d'Alene, a guy she'd liked from the moment she saw him, simply because he had a tattoo on his forearm that said, *I promise.*

When Val asked him what it meant, he said, I promise I never laid eyes on you. He stared her in the face, rolling a toothpick between lips and teeth, backed her up against his bedroom wall, kissed her deep, tongue and all. Think about it, he said. Nobody knows you're here. Am I right? I could take you. But am I making a move? Not on your life. Because I want to make sure I see you from time to time. That is the mark of a good retailer. Who knows. Maybe someday you'll grow to really like me.

Considering her position, she must have been nuts to pick up an illegal habit, still, she thought it was superior to developing an alcohol or man habit. Too many women she knew had been sucked into one or the other or both. That latter was probably the most toxic. All she had done was to drive to a classy blues pub she knew of in Spokane to ask a bartender where she could score. Definitely among her lower moments, but quite an adrenalin rush. The bartender exacted his price, gently but specifically. She'd gone into the backroom and let him fuck her against a row of silver kegs, walked back into the daylight in front of a row of men who knew exactly what she'd done, if their low whistles could be believed. Very high-risk behavior. The bartender was good-looking, and she hadn't been laid in a year. He had come inside her quickly, took her arm, pulled her to his chest and kissed her. She thought about AIDS. Of course she thought about AIDS. Thought about herpes and all the rest. Tugged her jeans back up, extended a hand. Not quite the same as doing it for money, but close. He wrote on a slip of paper, crumpled it, dropped it in her outstretched hand. Back in the car she opened it. You are beautiful, it said. A phone number with an Idaho area code. The word Kojak and an address in Coeur d'Alene. Val toyed with the idea of going home to Lewiston. She was high enough on her own endorphins. Yet as soon as she'd started the car and re-entered I-90 westbound, she took the first off ramp, heading east toward Coeur d'Alene. She hoped the bartender was kind enough to call ahead and tell Kojak she was on her way.

Weed. Cocaine dealers traded among the better-off middle-class drug users. Their clients tended to include judges, politicians, entrepreneurs. If you stepped over the line into the world of high-priced recreation, you risked running into people who could get you fired. Not so pot-smokers, who were predominantly lower-middle class, to her experience. Val normally restricted herself to a hit or two if someone else was providing it, underscored occasionally with a scotch. She wasn't about to let a tiny craving tweak her out of existence. Kojak turned out to be honorable, trustworthy, but she threw away his phone number after the third trip to his place, never let herself go back. You're a class act, he said, when she called to tell him what was up.

Val was waiting for Mitch to accompany her to 511 with Martin Tuor to his new bed in the St. Joe psych unit. The Fifth Floor, as it was known to citizens of the region, was often the entryway to the sedated purgatory of the state's mental institutions—and for this region, that meant State Hospital North and the prescription pen of Dan Weeks. The Fifth Floor was also a place for the imminently redeemable to take a break and reboot. A much better choice than shutting down people with Thorazine, as was common in Hospital North. Dan Weeks was old school, gravitated toward Thorazine. No one ever fully came back from it, and that would have been a sad case with Martin Tuor's potential for recovery.

Melinda joined them briefly at Martin's intake to act as recorder and witness his signature on his treatment plan. She swore later she wasn't going to be able to close her eyes without seeing his tight ass blooming from full hamstrings, called him Private Thighs. Makes me want to go to church, she said. Melinda otherwise had previously seemed beyond the men stage of herself, mostly focused on getting an online degree, yet she got misty over this pert little Aussie. Well *little* wasn't the case; Martin was built. *See?* Val whispered to the air. *We all have addictions.*

When he first walked up with Mitch, Val herself felt a note of surprise or recognition, even. Something about him made her take notice. She knew plenty of attractive men, so it wasn't just looks. What kept hitting her was that there was no hint of denial in him. He was clear about taking responsibility for stopping his meds. He'd had a seizure, was very worried about what this would do to his visa. Mitch spoke about a rider to his treatment plan, explaining as the three of them walked to the elevator and hit the button for the Fifth Floor. It's to be successive, Mitch said. Stay here at St. Joe a few days until we get the haloperidol stabilized, plus I want to try you on a new SSRI that singles out dopamine. It's called Wellbound. One of the happy side effects is that it will help you to quit smoking.

On the downside, it'll obliterate your sex drive. But that's not important now. What's important is getting you on your road again. We'll work out a medical visa. You can't travel until you're healthy. Our goal is to see that you are well taken care of.

Wellbound, Martin said. My home place back in Oz is called Outbound. Odd coincidence.

Val felt her heart stop, as if this were a personal slight. Magical thinking was one of Martin's predominant symptoms.

Oz? Mitch said.

Oz, Martin said. It's what we Aussies call it. No place else like it, and you've got to travel a long, hard road to get there, but once you do—paradise.

What Mitch did not say was that getting stabilized and healthy might open up the possibility of connecting with the half-brother who'd come looking for him and had appealed their first decision. Val, Mitch, Dan, and Matthew Seamus had talked it every way from Sunday, ultimately deciding again that now was not the time. Getting Martin's mind-set out of its dependent state using cognitive therapies could lead to him to normalize. A shock of that magnitude might cause him to spiral once more toward the wrong direction.

MAYA HE SÁPA

THE THINGS THEY TALKED about to avoid the chemistry between them.

They talked about the weather, the Northwest's wine industry, the local newspaper's benefits and inadequacies. The growing number of marmots along the levy; the way sea level isn't sea level anymore but nearly fifty feet lower than it was a thousand years ago when no one was counting. They talked about the homogenous faces of young actresses, how movies weren't as good as they used to be.

She was holding back from Martin, a truth she breathed into herself daily. After a dozen medical practitioners, a Seattle doctor at last figured her diagnosis: Epstein-Barr and chronic fatigue. A naturopath up north in Moscow explained the very mild heart failure that accompanied the syndrome, how a slight inaccuracy of the cardiac muscle kept her too tired to do much beyond answering phones in the farm bureau office six blocks from her house, to which she was unable to walk else she'd not have the energy to fulfill her duties. Some days getting to the car required crutches. Most days a cane.

Martin, on the other hand, appeared strong—muscles round and bulging from tank tops and cut-off shorts. He showed her time and again the awful photograph of his baby before he pulled the tube and then the one after, when the baby was dead, alluding to the difficulty this action caused him in years subsequent, but Maya hadn't detected a hint of failed fortitude, instead perceived him to be self-made, a man who could hold his own. Would he want her if he knew she was shored by herbs, calcium channel blockers, and tricyclics?

Otherwise, Martin had not shared too many details from his past, other than the fact that he was born and raised in Australia. What stories he did tell were rather wild. For example, back in the 1980s, after a year of living up by Winchester, he pulled all his possessions into a pit he dug with a camp shovel and set the pile ablaze: power tools, sofa, kitchenware, every stitch of clothing besides what he was wearing. When Maya stopped to think about it, however, she realized that she herself had had a few all-out yard sales, so perhaps it wasn't altogether unusual. It was purging. She felt free and clean afterward, made money enough to buy new. It was like rethinking herself.

If Martin wanted to know more about her, he wasn't asking. Meantime, Maya kept arriving at Java the Hut, kept stealing glimpses, kept hoping they would come together, certain when they did it would be thrilling and explosive. Cold nitroglycerin in a tropical jungle.

Stood the question, did two partial people really make a single whole one?

Part of the problem was that Maya and Martin rarely got to be alone. There was The Gang, as they called themselves, who congregated every morning to drink coffee, talk about politics, pontificate on the whys and wherefores of everything from homelessness to cigars.

His white Oldsmobile was parked in front of Java the Hut. The smell of pulp mill barely detectable, thinned by daybreak's haze. Four dogs—two black lab pups and two grown golden retrievers—were barking inside. He'd left the windows down six inches or so, through which four snouts jutted, licking and chewing the glass and yapping. He never left them home for fear of the damage they'd do, so they were used to this. Maya held a hand for each to lick and the four grew frantic over the attention. You poor babies, she said. Aren't you just so neglected?

The two pups pushed their heads outside, drool slipping down the glass like snail tracks. I know. I know, she said. One of the retrievers grabbed a pup by the nape, pulled it back inside, off-setting the bigger dog, causing all four to tumble across the seat to the floorboard in a chain reaction. The car rocked with the motion and the impact. Jeez Louise, Maya said, why anybody needs so many dogs.

Inside Java the Hut, Martin was seated in his usual spot—one of the dark green, overstuffed armchairs. He was ringed by The Gang: Jerry, Mike, Ron, Little Dennis, Robert, and Terri. Terri, in the middle of a divorce, was entertaining them with her ex's antics. Maya never had been married, although Martin had. I've been the crusher and I've been crushed, he told her once. At the time Maya thought he meant it as a warning to keep her distance.

The Gang consisted of mostly early retirees—Jerry and Mike from the pulp mill, Ron from the post office. Little Dennis was as his name ascribed—younger than the other men, smaller in stature. He always had a new plan for where to steer his life next. A musician hoping for discovery, his most recent scheme included Las Vegas and a shot at the big lights. She found herself glad to be part of them. For one thing, they never laughed at anybody's dreams. You go, they'd say, follow that star.

For indeed they each had. Ron and his wife Carol retired early to start a karate school. Carol was a former teacher with bright eyes and a fondness for hand-knit sweaters and fleece jackets bearing Pacific Northwest icons—moose and canoe and fir trees. Ron had a quadruple bypass, was proud of having dropped weight. You wouldn't know it, he told Maya, but delivering mail isn't enough. It looks like exercise, getting in and out of a truck, but it's not. City postmen? Maybe. But rural? Just move the truck rather than walk. Plenty of parking.

Ron liked to flirt, even in front of Carol, which made Maya squirm. Was that all Martin was—a flirt? No, there was his denim jacket, lying in one of the overstuffed chairs when everyone else was on hardwood seats (if Maya got her hands on those hardwood chairs, she'd paint them: butter yellows, purples, blues, with flower details and stems shot with leaf buds; jacquards; paisleys). Of course, she couldn't say what conversation sprouted from that little act of his, except when she pushed through the door, everyone cheered.

There she is, Ron said. Martin's saved the best seat for you. I might have insisted on it for Carol, except she's minding the shop today.

The moment must have been notable only to Maya, because the rest of them lapsed into their usual political discussion. Most of the democrats in Nez Perce county were seated right there. Lewiston, and, in fact, much of Idaho, was the land of a deliberate lack of deliberation when it came to politics. Martin was telling the story about how he loudly demanded free speech the time he'd been arrested for evading a police officer. He claimed if he'd committed no crime, he should be able to run from the *bobbies*, as he called them, if he wanted to. He'd never had so much as a speeding fine otherwise; he'd simply been walking down the street. The only reason the cop wanted to talk to him was because at that time he had long hair. They had a crime report and the perpetrator had long hair. Martin did have a stash of marijuana at home, but the officers didn't know that. As he told the story, they had no cause to interfere with his evening other than *the fact of his hair*.

Maya had spent hours listening to him go on about the arrest. He ranted about free speech, civil rights, Martin Luther King Jr., and being his namesake. She was kind enough not to point out the fact that Martin was born in Australia *before* Martin Luther King Jr. was famous.

Nobody cared that Lewiston harbored this little enclave of liberals. More likely it was perceived as a simple equation. There was, after all, Lewis-Clark State College sitting up there on Normal Hill. The sum of two addends—college town plus coffee shop. Of course nobody at the mill called it a college town. It was, by God, a work-hard/play-hard/good-old-boy kind of town. Most bars poured only Rainier, Budweiser, and Coors, and only weenie John Denver types drank Coors, plus a few women.

Moral of the story was that free speech was alive and well among the coffee-klatch gang. The showed up with weekly issues of *The Nation*, occasionally a *New York Times* or *Atlantic Monthly*. Only Mike's voice was discordant, conservative and sarcastic. He gave them something to argue against, once confiding to Maya that he didn't really harbor opinions, he just liked to rile people.

That is so mean, Maya had said.

Mike rolled his eyes, shook his head. Liberals, he said, as if the problem were genetic.

Maya was too busy with emerging affection to be serious about politics, although she listened with interest as Martin talked on about how governments had evolved into chess boards in which citizens were the playing pieces. Government was a man-thing to Maya. Men like Martin, objective outsiders who could hold to sentiment over time, were rare to her experience and not many were also nurturers. That's what a government should be, she thought—nurturing. She once found a book at the Goodwill called the *Chinese Book of Changes*. She loved to read the verses. They explained how a good leader at times has to hold back, be silent, or move forward slowly. Keeping in mind what was best for the people was the way to remain a leader and beloved. Plus, a good leader had to go down a great road of trials in order to solidify her or his humanity before being qualified to lead effectively, which, she decided, was why in the US actual leaders didn't go into politics. They were not prepared at that deep human level the way they should be, like Luke Skywalker and *Star Wars*. None of The Gang thought government had anybody's interests at heart, not because politicians weren't smart enough to connect enough dots. But because they didn't know which dots mattered to actual people—only which dots mattered to them.

A week later Maya was awakened by pain so severe she had to call an ambulance. Her muscles burned like they never had before, from the rounds of her jawbone to those in her calves, pain like a forest fire. She was conscious of its absence in her scalp's hair follicles, the creases on the soles of her feet, and the webs of her fingers. The rest of her musculature felt like it was being grated. She tried ibuprofen and vomited it. Vicodin with the same result. The phone was set to 911. Star one. The dispatcher answered. Maya whispered the details of her situation between gasps. The woman on the phone tried to soothe her. Hang on. Hang on, Maya. Stay with me. Get to the door and unlock it, but stay on the phone with me. The dispatcher was Beverly Sinclair. She knew Maya. Knew the drill. Breathe, Maya, honey. Don't hold your breath. Maya put down the phone to vomit in the wastebasket. Beverly was still there when she returned. The ambulance only has a few more blocks, honey. Maya heard satisfaction in Beverly's voice when she said, Okay now, darlin'. They're here. They're coming through the door.

The EMS guys were gentle, inquisitive. On a scale of one to ten? Last time you ate? How many times did you vomit? Pain in the chest? Numbness in your left side?

The fire, the fire, the fire, is all Maya meant to say, but she could not discern whether she truly spoke. *Please help me put out this fire!*

The lights overhead gleamed loudly. People were buzzing. Tiny little bees. It's okay, Sweetie. It's okay. We've got you, the nurse said. Then all was black. Maya was gone but she could feel her hair. Then she was back but someone had pulled the curtain; someone had hung a bag to her arm; the catheter pulsed between her legs. The nurse again. We've called your friend, she said, Martin. The number in your wallet. Your friend is on his way.

Martin doesn't know me, Maya whispered.

***

Martin did not come. Instead, Maya's landlord, Henry Bear, who was now coming to take her home. That she should have no family member to notify when she was lying in a hospital seemed an awful predicament. This was not lost on the nursing staff. They offered names of support groups. Talked about depression, the soothing nature of social contacts. Another social worker, a woman who introduced herself as Sabrina, tapped on the doorframe. Maya he Sápa? she said, I'm from Social Services. I'm here to talk to you about a loan from the county to pay your bill.

They began sleeping together in August. Martin started classes at Lewis-Clark State in September. By October they were discussing whether to move in together as a way to help each other with bills. Disability payments were small, less than a thousand a month for each of them, but if together they were only paying one rent, they'd be living in relative security for the first time in their combined lives. Maya's psychologist had argued it was too soon. Said starting college would be a lot for Martin to cope with emotionally, which, in his case, as Maya well new, could initiate another series of seizures. The discussion caused Maya to chastise herself, ask what had gotten into her, why she let herself fall for such a damaged guy in the first place.

She was lounging on the sofa with an open book on her chest envisioning their most recent encounter when the phone rang. The noise jolted her.

It was Terri. We're at Java, she said. Gang's all here.

Maya stifled a sigh. She didn't know if she were up to The Gang. Since her latest exacerbation, she was more easily exhausted. She had to work to take easy outs when she could, saving energy for cleaning the bathroom, dishes, reading the latest book on fibromyalgia, the latest addition to her list of diagnoses.

Terri was insistent. Come on, she said. A sugar-free mocha has your name on it.

I'd rather have an espresso brownie, Maya said.

Don't worry, Terri said. We'll protect you from yourself.

Maya considered it. I don't know if I can drive, Terri. I'm really tired, she said.

Worrywart, Terri said. I'm your taxi.

Maya tried a compromise. Why not just come here? I made tofu egg salad.

Heavy sigh, Terri said. Get your shoes on? You're about to blow a big surprise?

It wasn't her birthday. It wasn't anybody's birthday so far as she knew. Maybe Jerry got his recording contract. Her limbs felt weak and rotten. Whatever it was, there'd have to be a short end to it. She hung up the phone, got a sweater. Terri didn't waste a bit of time. Five minutes and there she was, standing on the step, tapping the screen door.

What on earth is going on? Maya asked, leaning heavy on the cane and doorframe.

You look like shit, Terri said, mirrored sunglasses reflecting Maya's hunched form back at herself. Maybe this isn't such a good day.

Come on. Good day for what? Maya asked.

Nope, Terri said, opening the door for Maya. Sworn secret.

They drove the short miles to Java the Hut, neither saying much.

You okay? Terri asked, parking, jamming the gearshift into place. Her car keys dangled from the ignition, a long jangle of them, fully six inches, Maya guessed, on a stained-glass owl key chain.

Isn't that hard on your ignition? Maya asked, pointing at the keys.

Okay, then don't answer, Terri said.

Once inside Java, it became clear something eventful was

happening. Martin had a huge smile on his face. Missing were Ron and Carol, who came walking up from the back entrance. What is happening here? Maya asked, lowering herself into a chair. What about classes, Martin?

Classes happen all the time, he said. Occasions don't.

He's going to propose to you, Ron said, reaching over to poke Maya in the side.

Shut up, Ron, everybody chimed in at once.

Nick, Java's owner and manager, walked over with a huge cake, square and built into a peaked roof. All that sugar. Maya felt light-headed just looking at it.

Why did he do it this way? Martin had leased a house. Even after all the nights of lists and arguments and discussions about emotions and their separate issues of health and mental health and how both their therapists were urging them not to join households until they were just a little further down the road to wellness. He had taken the decision into his own hands. From behind his back he handed her a bouquet of pink roses— stuffed into the middle of it an envelope of keys. A year's lease. Nick the manager lit the candles. Martin urged her to help him blow them out. Match sulfur tinged the air as he put his arms around her, taut and muscled next to her weak ones. Mike said she should take off her sunglasses, which she did, not realizing she still had them on. The scene had appeared golden up until then, the contrasting colors of reality briefly a shock. Mike flashed photo after photo as Martin and Maya, hands on the triangular cake cutter, sliced into the roof of the house, Nick the manager waiting with a stack of plates, the entire coffee shop applauding. Maya wasn't sure what she was agreeing to, since nobody, particularly Martin, had posed any question. He just stood there next to her in his tan and cut-offs and tank top and smile, putting forkfuls of cake into his mouth.

The dream came several nights in a row after Maya moved into the 4th Street cottage with Martin. She finally decided to write it down, in hopes that giving it concrete form would allow her to take control of it, stop it from invading her sleep. Not until she read it aloud to Martin, and they together watched the page burn to dark ashes in the kitchen sink, did the dream stop coming at night, still she couldn't stop thinking about it during the day.

Most images in the dream were black and white but some items were washed with fluorescent colors. She was sitting in a cabin she built on a foundation of stones from the walls of a canyon into which she was able to peer without moving from her chair, a canyon holding a white-capped, purulent river. A spring river. On the sky was written a long paragraph in cursive: *The banks were shiny wet and green with moss and lichen, lace-limbed bushes with tiny flowers, pink, white, lemon-yellow teacups and saucers of wild daffodils, draped willow buds. The sound of the water was more like thousands of sweeping brooms. It felt like the ocean and midnight air in summer.* Looking up the canyon wall from the room where she sat, she could see through the leaves of great oaks to young ponderosas clinging to rock outcroppings like babes to a mother. She saw the precarious search of root tips under that crust of soil, hoping spring rain would slow, wouldn't wash them tumbling with their tree-host mothers into the river below.

Then the scene changed: she was staring under the cabin's eave at a waxen hornets' nest, a ghost from another year, thinking she should get the broom and sweep it down before spring. Without warning, the nest came to life, and a world of hornets swarmed, which woke her. Each night was the same. Martin was asleep on his side, his back turned. The walls and ceilings of their tiny bedroom, painted a pretty shade of white and the gauzy curtains overly long and ballooning against the lovely wood floor calmed her. No pictures filled the wall's empty spaces, but Martin was taking an art class. Give me time, he said, when she talked about wanting decoration on them. Just give me a little more time.

***

You could consider getting up and trying to move on from
it.

It was the same argument. Maya was standing by the sink
in her bath slippers and pink housecoat. She had a doctor's appointment and was trying to get ready. Martin was sipping a
joint and a cup of coffee, fuming on some perceived injustice
inflicted on him at ILC in the past. His case manager was trying to strike a bargain with him involving his meds to keep
him on his SSI money. Martin wanted to take himself off the
meds again, but the official in charge of his case, Danny Weeks,
had put it clear and simple in a letter. No meds, no money. The
plan was to remain as it had always been: to wean Martin off
services and back into independent life, but he had to prove
himself first. He had to remain compliant and symptom-free
for two years. He'd never been able to stick with his medica-
tions more than six months. Along with the letter was a copy of
records showing how many medication and case management
visits he'd missed. Even though he was still in classes at Lewis-
Clark and was handling that, his bosses at A & B Foods were
getting to him, so he bought weed, had picked back up a beer
habit. Maya hated coming home and seeing Martin at the table
with his fist around a quart of beer.

Things had gotten worse, she felt, when the Independent
Living Center closed. Now Martin was being monitored as a
Hospital North outpatient. He had an RN case manager, which
meant going to Public Health for a weekly injections of a drug
called Haldol. Which was stupid, Martin said, over and over,
because Haldol wasn't a seizure medication. Things had also
gotten worse after Martin was arrested this most recent time.
It was nothing, a misunderstanding, as it always was, but he
had been drinking on the levy yet again, and drinking on the
levy was not allowed. Even though he didn't stay overnight,
and he was never charged, still the police hooked him up and

took him in. They wouldn't let him have his backpack with the pictures and baby cap in it, which caused Martin to cry so hard they thought he was going to have a nervous breakdown. This led to him being placed on Prozac, which he took for a few days and then flushed down the toilet. What is the difference between beer and pills? he said. I grew up with one, and it was good enough for everyone I knew. Fuck your pills, America. You can bloody well keep them.

One day she decided to go to the library to see what she could find about Haldol, about seizures, and fibromyalgia. It was amazing, the Internet. A constellation of tiny libraries. Haldol was not for seizures but for hallucinations and schizophrenia. He was quite changed when he first came back from the Fifth Floor, and no seizures, but over the months he became self-centered and verbally volatile towards Val Corsica and the Independent Living Center crew. He used to love *playing snooker with the crazies*, as he called it. He'd go several times a week after work or classes. Going to play snooker with the crazies, he'd say, in his Australian accent, kissing Maya passionately *for luck*, like he was happy in his life.

Then ILC closed. Sometimes when Martin got really morose, she'd try convincing him to go dig around in in the yard a bit, pull a few weeds, plant the salsa garden he was always talking about. He'd accuse her of thinking him a *bad egg*, after which he generally left and came back with a six-pack. She didn't know, really, if she should just give up or not, but they'd turned the little house into such a lovely place, painting and pulling up carpet and sanding floors with the landlord's blessing. They'd gotten permission even to put in a skylight and widen the window casings so they were big enough to hold plants. Martin had done all the work himself with salvaged materials. He was a wonderful carpenter.

He talked about going back to Australia, which, she knew, was one of his treatment goals. His therapist thought he needed to make peace with the circumstances of his childhood, the death of his son, his divorce. Martin refused to see these as issues, nor would he admit to any of his actions as problems. Sometimes when Maya awakened to him sleeping next to her, when she could see the funny, smart guy he was when they met, she tried to imagine what it would be like to leave your birthplace, just because you held curiosity about another country. One time they went for a walk on the river path, and Martin turned a three-sixty looking at the Snake and Clearwater River canyon and confluence, saying under his breath, Crikey. Australia with water and a wallet. And I could have gone any other bloody place.

From what she was reading, Haldol was an *anti-hallucinogen*. Her stomach quit at Haldol's common usage: treatment of paranoid hallucinations and primary schizophrenia.

Eventually, Martin moved out. Terri told Maya she knew a girl who dated an Aussie and that Aussie men only care about their *mates*, meaning male friends. In the weeks leading up to leaving, Martin became more and more restless. Shaved his beard, grew his beard. Mowed the lawn, didn't mow the lawn until the weeds were so thick and tall the neighbors complained. Took out a section of garden, put in a section of garden. Bought a computer, sold a computer. Came home late and slept on the couch. Sometimes didn't come home at all. Always a certain scent following him. Not like sex, exactly, but as if he'd been where there was smell-good in the air. No alcohol or cigarette smoke, so it wasn't bars. But something hung on him. Some change.

He started sitting over his cereal with the *Lewiston Morning Tribune*, not sharing the news. Watching TV less. Cleaning his messes. Doing laundry. Keeping his journal. Filling out line after line with a black roller ball pen pulled from a box of a dozen, bought at Staples. Maya had never bought a box of pens before. Pens were something you accidentally stole from the counter at the hardware store—cheap ballpoints with metal plungers that chipped at the barrel tip and clotted and leaked ink. But Martin bought a dozen black roller balls along with a cloth-bound book with blank pages. He carried both with him as faithfully as people carry Bibles, so faithfully Maya never got a chance to look in it.

One night after he failed to come home she noticed that some items were missing from the house. A couple of paintings and trinkets she knew Martin liked. A few books. She sat on the sofa waiting through the night and into the dawn, the knowing like a little flame: *he left*. She bade herself not look until the sun came fully up, but when it did, she went to his closet. Every thread and button was gone.

MARTIN TUOR

DON'T GO, MOM! No! Don't go! He stood at his bedroom windows watching her leave, the bedroom in the house at the rise of the slight hill in the caravan park his parents built, which kept them and him and his three sibs in tucker and shoes. Piotr, the eldest, who at nearly sixteen, stood taller than their dad; Annalesa, the next eldest and fifteen; himself, Martin, thirteen in March, and Barney, almost six, still the littlest of kids, still hugging the rug that saw them four through teething and the sleep terrors.

She was carrying a packed grip, it contents unknown to Martin. All he did know was what he saw on her: a thin cotton dress he'd watched her sew herself on the treadle — white with pale flowers and dots that to him made his mother look like an angel; a pale blue sweater hooked over her forearm like a partial sleeve; a straw hat, its brim just wide enough to keep the sun off her eyes; a pocketbook, also straw, dyed nearly to the same blue as her sweater. This was the last sight Martin had of her, her slender frame softened by a bit of pudginess, walking down the lane, curious tenants standing on curlicue porches made by Pops, waving, perhaps wondering, but none speaking. Whether she carried Martin's photo or the heart-shaped piece of greenstone he wrapped in tissue and gave her for her birthday, he did not know, but for certain he wished it.

It was November again, spring already, gorse yellowed and wisteria and rose-of-sharon in the gardens pinked, the bright red kangaroo paws in the bush apt to be unfurling. Martin wondered what he did to bring on her leaving. He tried to give his bedroom a good clean often enough, but it was a chore and chores kept him from his preferred pastime — playing outdoors in the dirt with the other kids and the dogs. Finding rocks and shells, sometimes an interesting dead insect or bit of shed snakeskin. Dried toad, chook and maggie feathers. Sometimes a flattened Cherry Ripe or wad of tree gum, hardened to preserve his teeth marks. Shriveled apple cores hooked to a string for hanging from a tree to attract bees. The Chinese coin with a hole in its center he carried for luck. On occasion a shilling, which he would save until he had threepence, in which case he'd buy himself into the new outdoor theatre of an evening, else the threepence fall through a tear in his pocket and its advantages be lost. A chap could stand to lose a shilling through a pocket hole, but if he got to the point of threepence, he thought himself better off to spend it on something memorable. His mother began refusing to do his wash when she found all on the same Monday morning a dried tiger snake, a pair of blood-edged ears off some small creature, stabbed through with karroo thorns, the bushes of which he and the Cleary boys had one day found suddenly—where months before they had not been—a boy-sized jungle spreading from the Jelico side of his exploration boundaries and into which the three of them regularly ventured and from which he regularly received a supply of scratches requiring the application of stinging red iodine; if his mother knew about the injuries, she would say simply, Stay out of the karroo thorn, then, so he didn't tell her, until he heard his Pops reading an official post warning about collecting and destroying the seed pods of karroo thorn if found on their property; in the end, him, his pops, and Nate Cleary and the Clearly boys banded together to harvest and make a fire with them, figuring to do their loyal part for the state of Western Australia.

Even still, he tried to do his share of the cleaning, since he felt bad for his mom, since the wiping task was endless from the air constantly being speckled with dirt off the Drury Road. It clogged his bed netting, collected on the side table and frog lamp, the heap on the floor, his clothing, the rug under which he dreamt at night. Lately his mom had begun to claim the dust and flies were killing her, the way they kept her walking around with a damp cloth to every counter and flat surface. Each evening during the worst months of it, she made Martin change the whirligigs of flypaper hanging in every room.

The painting. At first Martin nor his sibs nor their dad thought bad of it. It started a number of summers back, as soon as the wet let up, Mom waking up one morning shouting orders, wanting the wallboards peach instead of their longstanding green, mopboards and door and window sashes amber instead of white. Which was all fine and dandy, since the green in all the rooms over the years had been scrubbed through to the shiplap, the mopboards and moldings chipped and pocked by years of kids banging them with sticks and hard-shoed feet.

Problem was, Mom decided she wanted them scrubbed paint-free with grit paper. So while the older kids got the job of pulling boards loose from the plaster with the leveraging tool, Martin was given a tack hammer with which to tap the nails out. The trick, Pops told him, was tapping the nail hard enough without bending it or snapping the molding. I'm giving you the job, he said, because you have greater patience than your brother Piotr.

Before he got to nail number three, Martin had knocked himself off balance. Stepping backward to right himself, he managed to spear his foot, thanks to a freshly removed board Piotr had casually tossed on the floor in Martin's path, on purpose, because he was a bastard.

Within a day of stepping on the nail, Martin fell feverish and upset his tea, at which his mom and dad dug out the wound, stuffed it with black pepper, tied it with cloth strips, and dosed him with castor oil for the toxins and Enos to put oxygen in his blood.

According to Annalesa, when Martin didn't awaken the next morning, but laid there blacked out and white-hot with red streaks barreling up his leg toward his heart, Pops carried him to the Vanguard and the family climbed in for the ride to Doctor Wallace's infirmary—or Dr. Wallaby, as little Barney termed it—who rattled Martin out of the sedan and onto a gray-rugged table. He reckoned he was in for the needle. Martin loathed having his knickers pulled down in public, which was the unfortunate circumstance since Dr. Wallace's office was puny, the exam table shimmied into the corner, the framed drape on wheels partitioning the table from the front window, and nothing more.

The thing Martin remembered was the sweat in his eyes. *A good sign.* The words floated in the air. The mercury in the blood pressure machine rose in response to the doctor pumping its squeaky bulb. Dr. Wallaby. Let's hold our panic. Instead, let's look forward to finding an end to the young whip's troubles, he said. Leaning into Martin, the smell coming from the man's mouth like that of a new icebox, he said, Not more than a spider bite. Give us a minute, little mate. Have you right as royal in no time.

The man stood straight again, stepping closer to Martin's parents, pointed to his own leg and groin, whispered. Mom sucked in her breath, to Martin in slow motion, the bowl between her collarbones and the base of her neck sinking deeper into its pink tissues. *Pinker*, Martin thought. *Getting pinker and pinker.*

Lockjaw! His mother's gasped repetition of the doctor's words.

Pinker! Getting pinker and pinker! Martin heard the yell as if from the other side of the room. Pinker! Pinker! Pinker! He tried to wish aloud for the screaming to stop and Annalesa and Mom to stop their bawling, but all his voice would say was, Pinker! Pinker and pinker!

Then the cold stab into his bared hip, medicine going in and in, the sound of the nurse cooing, padding towels beneath him, the quince smell of alcohol in the water basin. *Pinker! Pinker!* Martin tried to sit up and ask for a drink of water. Pinker! his voicewhispered as the nurse put her hands to his shoulders and pushed him back down onto the cot.

Shshh, little blarneystone, shshh, she said, in a brogue like that of the tenant family, the Nathan Clearys, while the alcohol water fell over Martin's body like sugar, cool dark, and mean as petrol. Martin fell and fell into it. He heard the swish of his mother's cotton dress as she sunk to the floor, the sound of the mint-and-ocean smell of his father's cologne moving in an earthward direction to grasp her.

But how can you hear a smell? he asked the nurse.

Shshh, wee one, she said. Shshh now.

***

Martin figured that to be when she began being pissed at him, his stepping on that molding board with the nails up-turned the way he did, interrupting her plans, even though he did recover, except for a bubble of tissue like a crucifixion scar on top of his foot.

He's Jesus! He's Jesus! Piotr and little Barney—one just as tow-headed and sun-brown as the other, clearly sandwiching Martin's between-them age and head of dark hair—loved to run yelling around the caravan park. Once, after Martin's accident, the three patched together a cross from an old creosote rail and a piece of rafter from a shearing shed, a splintered ghost from the days when the park's land was checkered with paddocks and chutes. People swore they could still smell and hear, late of a hot night, the blood and bleats of ram jewels being nipped and ewes when their lambs were sold to the feed butcher because they were born dead or deformed. A story was told of a lightning strike that galled an entire flock and the station manager had to put the herd down. Scorched them to leather on the hoof, so it was said. Stories like that floated around, clinging to the brains of people. It was listening to the telling that pleased folks, Martin believed, because it made them imagine pictures to go with the words. After all, people paid to go to movies. Which drove him to instruct Piotr and Barney in creating the crucifixion story, inviting every kid with tuppence to come look at Martin's feet. That he only had one scar and Jesus had two didn't seem to bother them. They plopped down their coin, sweat- and dirt-smeared. Nathan Cleary's youngest son, Nate-Mate, everyone called him, swore he could hear an angel's voice coming from Martin's scar, and Martin thought that to be the thing that sent his Mom packing, because the moment she first walked up on the mob of them sitting beneath the cross, Martin with his foot propped on an upturned pail and Nate-Mate's curly brown head bent over talking to it like it was the shortwave, she balled her fists and screamed, Get out! Get out! And take that bloody tree down!

Of course, no one moved so much as a toe. Everyone knew the story of turning green walls peach and putting kids to handling dangerous things—hammer, leverage tools, and such— and knew Cherise's reputation for being one berry short of a bucket (as Nate-Mate explained was *his* mother's way of describing her) and so stayed seated at the foot of the cross.

Their inaction crazed her further, so that she ran to the house screaming for Martin's father, who came out with galluses dangling, in his singlet, baring his shoulder knobs, asking the group gently to please tear on home. Martin and Piotr pushed the cross to the ground and carried it through what Pops told them used to be a shearing paddock, which had become the caravan park activity grounds with bench tables and rope swings. She didn't like having to think about Jesus except on Christmas, I reckon, Martin's father said.

Then the day came when his mom opened a card from people called The McMurtreys. They're coming in, Edmonds! she said. Lord god. All these years later. From the United States. Russell and Jeanne McMurtrey. They're coming in!

***

Martin was six when he first heard the words, *United States*. His dad spoke them right alongside words like *Yanks* and *bas-*

tards. He heard over and over a word called *Korea*. Like it might be a radio show, his mom and dad every night leaned over the wireless, listening, Pops sometimes shouting, his mom with a handkerchief to her nose. What it all meant—as with nearly all questions—he could not make himself ask. Men could be seen leaving, pacing themselves down the Drury Road and past the Outbound, some walking up the lane to inquire about a spot of water. Some eventually returning, including Nate Cleary, Barry Gibson, and the Ferguson brothers, up to a year or more after they'd left, all of whom who came whenever Pops needed help toting things about or, once, to stand the great water tower on its four beetle legs.

He did try to ask his mom, who only said, Pops can tell it best.

His dad only said, Boy, it'll just give you bad dreams. The world is dreadful and beautiful. You'll learn that quick enough.

As was his habit, Martin closed himself in his room to look at his rock and shell collection, bits he had no names for but that he made up himself. There were points and diggers and shark's tooth. This last name he got because he heard some road men who were sleeping in one of the caravans talking about some bloke having been killed by a shark north of Port Augusta. It was a type of white rock he could never crush no matter how hard he tried to smash it, one he liked very much.

In the autumn of 1966, the year after Mom left, Piotr's troubles started. Martin had just turned fourteen. Piotr was sixteen. Annalesa was still fifteen and little Barney going on seven.

One night the family was awakened by Piotr screaming from the lounge, where he had taken to sleeping on the pull-out in the months prior to Mom's going away, leaving Martin alone in the bedroom they had always shared.

There's a bloke under there! A bloke is breathing! Piotr yelled.

Martin went running, half-sleeping, toward the noise, and found Piotr on the lounge under a roo pelt Pops had purchased for pennies from the taxidermy in Gillagong, because some bloke never came to retrieve it, a stark, hairy thing none of them could bear as a rug but Piotr.

They're too ugly off the roo, Annalesa had said, after Pops carried it in and draped it across the lounge.

When Martin tried to pull back the pelt, Piotr wailed and held it to his chin, looking Martin square and full on, the whites of his eyes showing, crazed the way Mom had looked the time he and the Clearys tried to force the Clearys' cat into a pail of water dosed with purple dye powders Nate claimed to have pilfered from the dry goods store in Denton.

Bloody hell! Martin said, and Pops didn't even mark the vulgarity. Too busy staring at the stranger that was Piotr. Annalesa—who just that summer had grown norks and started wearing minis and mascara, the latter of which most of the time was mostly a smear blacking her eyes like a lemur—arrived in her baby doll pajamas. Close behind her was little Barney, heading off soon enough to the Peabody District School, leading Pops by the hand—a familiar arrangement since Mom left—to see what was causing the ruckus.

Piotr was big as a grown man, taller even than Pops, and where always before he was wide at the belly and hips, now the belly and hips had switched places with the shoulders and chest. He'd taken to buying *Atlas Quarterly* and built himself a pair of barbells out of cement block, which he regularly hefted in various repeating patterns. His muscles were bold as Nate Cleary Sr.'s and he was prone to showing them off, going about in singlets and cuffed pants he ordered from America. Levis, he called them. Pops was constantly on him about it, a son of his, going about like a drover. Piotr had learned the vulgar jab of the middle finger and used it on Pops at every turn. Martin couldn't fathom its meaning, until he finally asked, and Piotr said, You bloody prawn, it's me ass finger, isn't it?

This didn't clarify things for Martin at all, so he consulted Nate Cleary Jr. who said, It's about something a mate does to his missus. What makes the joeys come out.

Martin recollected his Mom round and sweating just before little Barney arrived. Still not satisfied, he asked Pops, who said, Sit down, I reckon. Now listen. And for once don't tell the world about it.

Intrigued with the information, Martin felt disgusted at his older brother, for turning such a logical thing into meanness against their dad.

Pops moved in close to the lounge and tried to lay a hand on Piotr's head in the way Mom would have, to see if he was fevered. Piotr screamed, Bloody Jesus! Pops withdrew as if he'd spotted a viper, took a second step back, the bones of his shoulders poking through his skin. Martin noticed the hair gone white on his dad's chest. He'd never seen it before, with the man working constantly out in the full-on sun and browned tip to tip, but here in the milk-light of the lounge room, Pops looked dim, his muscles string-like, powerful hand shivering. Martin knew something he hadn't before noticed: Pops missed Mom. He wondered if Mom had taken on the same level of oddness.

Piotr wailed like a stuck boar again. He's under the lounge! He's breathing under the lounge! Bloody hell! Get him out before he kills the mob of us! He'll kill the mob of us!

Martin thought his brother had taken on a demon-like texture himself, like the one in his mom's Holy Bible, a picture in which Jesus had slain a devil by spearing him with a sword. He could easily imagine Piotr growing horns and scales, eyes glowing red. The illusion faded in the lamplight Annalesa turned on at Pops' behest, so that he might inspect beneath the lounge, which was—visible to all but Piotr—vacant as the tea shelf, now that Mom was gone and Pops had switched to buying burlap sacks of coffee beans to roast and grind. Martin squeezed his eyes shut several times and opened them again, trying to blur the picture of Piotr with long, pointed fangs, blood dripping.

Indeed, blood did appear at the corners of his brother's

mouth, smeared by a hand dragged across the cheek. Later, Dr. Wallaby, as the entire family privately still called him, assured Martin Piotr had merely bitten his tongue.

Martin, Pops said, crank up the wireless. See if you can raise the constable. Tell him to bring the medicos.

NOOOOO! NOOOOO! Piotr moaned, rearing off the pullout, throwing aside the pelt. I'll bloody kill him, I will. I'll bloody kill the son of a bitch and the lot of you! he whispered through his teeth, the blood now in full drops falling off his chin.

Annalesa covered her face with her hands and began sobbing silently, running from the room, baby dolls flipping to show the patterns of her underpants over her behind. Little Barney moved behind Pops' legs, thumb to mouth, wide-eyed and simpering.

Martin walked over and switched on the overhead lamps. Everyone turned to look: Pops, little Barney, Piotr. Piotr's demon must have vanished with the brighter light, since his horrible wailing ceased. Piotr appeared small, withered, green about the face, eyes glazed. He reached up to wipe froth from his lips, smiled, asked Pops to dim the light so he might get some sleep.

Out in the yard, the moon nearing three-quarters cast the same milk white over the park and the play yard as had been in the lounge room. A thought stuck in Martin's brain he couldn't bring forth. Something had been decided.

Ooh-ess-ah, he said to the lean-to, to the board he had to pry loose to find his stash of tobacco. *USA*, he wrote in the dust. He might only be a kid, but his decision was solid as rocks. No matter how long it sat across the oceans waiting, Martin's future was in the US of A.

***

The benefit to being in America was that strangers right off wanted to start a conversation just to hear Martin speak. People were comics, urging him to *say one more thing*, rewarding him with food and grog. He learned right off that he could strike up a conversation with a sheila just by saying good day.

It was not a week since he arrived, numb from a trail that started with kicking up the dust of Drury Road against the sound of Pops cursing and Annalesa keening. Days perched on a cushioned bench, smelling of dust and horse hair, leaning into the waddle of the Indian Pacific rail train, which in recent years had been extended such that it ran clear from Perth to Sydney.

Finally, to the rotation of airplanes from Sydney to New York, the first flight of his life. Already he'd eaten free for the taking *pirogues* and *slices*. In both cases, two days apart and on two different avenues, vendors launched from alongside steaming metal carts the same booming promises about the grade and quality of their goods. Of course, it went without saying, it was the smell of frying spice and meat that drew people in, including himself. He no sooner had walked up to give an order than both chaps called out, *Well, if hit idn't Crahk-o-dile Dun-day*, after which one chap described the price of Martin's meal as, *Hitson me taday Mistah Dun-day*. The second sounded something like, *Fagitabowtit. Tsonnaouse.*

People had been throwing the words *Crocodile Dundee* at Martin the entire week and in each instance he stood staring at the mouth of whomever was speaking, unable to think of a reply, at which the first vendor, a dark, mustachioed man, flashed his meat cleaver and said, That's not a *knoif*. This is a *knoif*. Not bad, hey *mate*? smiling widely, as if he were in front of an audience and very proud of himself. Martin didn't know why he should care for the chap's blade, a tool of his trade, but when a bloke is smiling and offering your tucker for free, it softens you and you give him the benefit of expecting him to be all right.

Meanwhile he tried not to think about being alone in a new country. Had he stayed in Jelico and kept at the Outbound with Pops, there would be no question about his days. A regular working bloke. Every December a new crop of families on holiday whose kids skinned elbows and foreheads flying off the twirl-around, knocked their breath loose on the seesaws, ran crying to the rented caravans to smear snot-noses on the walls and lounge, which Martin had to soap off.

Which brought him to the raising of little Barney. That had taken something out of all of them, trying to make sure he turned out. Ended up he was the best of them, twenty-one, done with his education at uni. As had the sustained mild possibility of Martin resuming with Jennie Kay, who turned her back once and for all when it became clear there was no medical cure for Martin's seizures. Then there had been those years taking care of Pops, with more ahead, who had come down with heart failure while pushing the mower not too long after Jenny Kay packed her grip. Put the old man in Sisters of Hollywood Hospital in Perth for a fortnight.

Once Pops was declared sturdy enough to return to his previous habits, Martin decided to make known his decision to give in to his long-held urge for America. Annalesa and Pops both stopped their morning cuppa mid-sip. Pops set his teacup down on the table to say, Well, hurry on. Reckon to watch every haired ass in my family walk off down the Drury Road.

After which commenced the yelling, screaming, strop-swinging craze that marked their days since Mom walked off. Pops lashed the strop at the fence, a gum tree. First the puff of dust from her departing feet, he said, ratcheting his shoulder again, and again. Then Piotr off to the funny farm, then the newborn not even making it out of the hospital crib. Then Jenny Kay took her leave. By the time he'd worn himself out, the sweat streaming and the tears and the sobs, his voice a whisper, he said, You'd think if there be a God he would sure as hell send a big sign to Jenny Kay, at least. To make her want another try.

As it was, a day later, Martin had instead found himself squatting beside Drury Road to spell his bones from walking. He had pulled out the tissue-covered knit cap from Sisters of Hollywood incubator room and the pair of Polaroids showing his son Michael's eyelids closed gray and soft. When he got to Perth, he figured to buy a flat jarrah box to house the items, hopefully guarantee them safe passage to America.

Martin lay on his bunk at the hostel night after night, missing home and Jenny Kay, wondering how a chap travails a flood to help a mob of strangers, meets a pretty misplaced sheila of a Yank thirty-four to his twenty-one, marries her, sets up housekeeping and goes to work in the cane to bloom calluses until he doesn't recognize his own hands, loves the sheila whenever the two come within a stone's toss of the sheets, a year or two later planting not one babe but three, only to have the first two come out as small, bloody lumps within a fortnight of the sheila's belly starting to round, the third born strangled by the very cord of life that fed and kept him all that time, with a hole in his tiny heart, starting and ending his existence with needles in his scalp and tubes strung through his body, breath forced by a bellows. Their baby was born crook only days before he died.

After which came hours of sitting in a rocking chair holding Jenny Kay as if a baby herself, next to that little bloke in his clear tub, a tiny box of a world that kept him warm as the womb, the sound of all those machines, the sheep's bleat of the heart monitor, that little uneven rhythm going just right once in a while, falling off, then picking up again. All the while Jenny Kay sitting on Martin's lap crying and crying, his own tears a flood just as hazardous as any Deadhorse Creek could think up. He leaned in to smell her hair, hoping to hold that scent of lavender and womanness forever, knowing full well the end had come. Jenny Kay was solid, especially for a sheila, but once they pulled Baby Michael's breath tube, she'd be a goner. She'd never stay married to him, and if she did, their days would be long and still. Might as well cut their two throats, for all the chances they had of getting on together.

It was Martin's idea to be the one to pull out the tube. The doctor would disconnect it, and Martin would pull it out of Michael's lungs. Jenny Kay said she couldn't stand to be there, lifted the wee chap, blankets and all, from the incubator for one last hug and to put him to the breast. He never had fed from it, of course, hadn't the strength, but day after day she had put his mouth to the nipple, nonetheless, to watch his little mouth begging like a chick after the worm. Then the nurse would hook up the electric pumping machine. After the pale blue nourishment grew from a puddle in the bottom of the bottle to twenty or thirty milliliters, Jenny Kay would pick up the wee chap again and put a rubber nipple between his lips. The little bloke strangled every time, at which point she'd hold off, then run the whole routine again. She kept it up for that period of days, Jenny Kay trying to prove Baby Michael was all right and healthy and going to stay that way. It was a lie, same as the way Martin soothed himself to sleep at night as a kid by telling himself his Mom was just on holiday, would any moment come walking back up Drury Road, same as she left.

The proof otherwise came by way of fact: the lad dropped from a kilo and a half at birth to a kilo after four days. He's starving to death, the lumbering, red-haired Scot of a doctor said on Sunday morning. We can continue as is until his systems start to fail, or we can discontinue the therapies and let him nod off.

It was a point of pride to Martin that they had at least given the little bloke his try. It was that pride that led him to say to Jenny Kay as she lay whimpering into his shoulder in bed that night, It's time he went his own way.

She nodded her agreement, and the two got dressed and went back to hospital until daylight, holding and rocking Baby

Michael for the time he had remaining. The nurses must have understood what they meant to do, for they made no interference. They merely dimmed the light in the nursery and let them be.

Martin didn't know how long he sat after Jenny Kay passed the baby over to him and walked away. He thought for a brief bit it was his Mom with her satchel in hand, and sure enough, while he was sitting there, a big, dark-haired nurse named St. Louis strode in to check on him and ask if he were related to a Cherise Tuor she had known in Sydney some years back. Unusual last name, you know, she said. Swiss.

Aye, Martin had said, that'd be my Mom, I'd expect.

Nurse St. Louis looked toward the ceiling, as if considering whether to say more, but didn't. Martin asked if she'd be a mate and take a photograph of him holding Baby Michael, and a few minutes later she came back with an Instamatic Polaroid, the kind that spit out a picture right away, and snapped it. Martin pulled loose the swaddling and kissed Michael on the chin, then leaned upright, supporting the baby at the neck and lower back. Michael's eyes under closed lids were huge, the knit hospital cap covering a cranium larger than his face. The lower lip was full and pouting, pointed at the philtrum, the skin of the cheeks peachy smooth but flat and pale, like the pallor of one long imprisoned. Michael's chest rose and fell with the movement of the machine, but, of course, the developed photograph didn't capture that.

I'm ready, Martin said. Are you ready little chap? Nurse St. Louis walked away and blew her nose. Ah, now. It's all right, isn't it, Little Michael? It's only the grown-ups crying. Not you, little charmer. You're too brave a bloke.

Nurse St. Louis asked Martin again whether he was ready, to which he nodded yet again, the well of courage and fortitude high in him at that moment, like a house full of daylight, at which point Nurse St. Louis opened a nearby doorway and said something to the bloke inside, who came with her to the respirator, both swishing with the movement of starched cotton, then the sound of two pair of shoes stopping, and the metallic interruption of an electrical circuit.

That's all it took. Martin's breath froze within that last sound. Meanwhile Nurse St. Louis handed a fat syringe to the doctor, who used it to undo whatever was holding the respirator inside Michael's throat. Nurse St. Louis then lay Martin's hand atop the strange roundness of the tubing. *Like a stiff willy.* Then the resistance gave, the tube dislodged itself along with a bit of Michael's saliva and a smear of gunk. He coughed and sucked hard at the hospital atmosphere, startled as a landed fish, and Martin panicked and shook. The boy's cry creaked like he was coming to life, his face at first limp, then enraged. Maybe he was going to live!

Then a series of words pushed themselves to the forefront of Martin's brain, loud as if the tiny chap had actually spoken. *Never give up*, the words said. *Never give up*. Little Michael and Martin sucked wind into their lungs simultaneously.

Did you hear that? Martin asked Nurse St. Louis.

Hear what, Sweets? she asked.

Him! The kid! Clear as church bells! Martin said.

Of course, she said. Go right along now. Of course.

Nurse St. Louis snapped another photograph of Michael lying across Martin's lap. Martin hoped she caught the hint of a smile and the peacefulness.

He looks peaceful, doesn't he? he asked, the ammonia smell of emotion rising in his nose, his face quivering. Then the melt to tears.

Yes, he does, Mr. Tuor, Nurse St. Louis said. Yes, he does. Peaceful as wheat.

***

It rained most of every day of the first week in New York, gray and meager. Each drop hit the sidewalk with a brief, dulled twinkle, casting back the streetlights which were lit up even though it was daytime. Sitting on the steps under the hostel's canopy, Martin looked for the center of the splat before it disappeared, staring himself cross-eyed, then looking up and through traffic to focus. A chap who'd introduced himself as Wilhelm the night before skipped down the steps to sit. What do you think of New York? Wilhelm asked, his Swiss homeland burring the edges of his speech in a way familiar, thanks to Martin's Mom and Pops' origins.

Where I'm from, you'd count it lucky, every drop, Martin said.

I suppose, Wilhelm said, combing fingers through his hair. You given to brew?

Martin laughed. If you're asking do I know my way through a tinnie, the answer I'd have to say is, yes. That's a way to get to know a bloke. Yes, I've been known to lift a tinnie.

Tinnie, Wilhelm said. There's a word. A rose is a rose, or so some Brit once said.

Mom was a hand with the rose bushes, but I can't say about anybody else, Martin said. My duster's on the rail there. If you'll hand me it, we can be on.

Wilhelm reached to hand Martin the caped bush coat and stopped to examine it. I suppose a working man would favor this, he said. Might make you stand out in the US, though.

It's but a sheepman's coat, Martin said.

Just a note, Wilhelm said.

Aye. Just a note, Martin said, pulling his arms through the sleeves and flipping the collar against the dampness. It's old as rocks. Two blokes yesterday tried to purchase it, and in the hostel somebody took it off my hook in the middle of the night. We near went to cuffs when I went to get it back. I've had to make it my pillow.

The two stepped onto the landing without another word,

until Wilhelm pointed to a pub called The Munich Room and said, My homeland. Mind?

The rain had grown more delicate. Martin flattened a palm skyward, to which Wilhelm said, Yes? Martin meant the gesture as ambivalence, not surrender, but before he could address it, the bloke had descended the stairway, his hand on the knob of the pub's dark door, out of hearing range or not listening or both. Martin experienced the short discomfort of chagrin he felt when Pops used to order him to chores, swallowed it, decided to save himself from his own habit of making a world affair of his private emotions.

Inside The Munich was as dark as its door, but he quickly adjusted. The bare light from the outside passed through an old lead-glass window, stained from years of tobacco smoke. The only blokes in the building were the barkeep and a trio of blond men with a card game going and a stack of poker chips between them. Wilhelm hiked himself to a stool, looked at Martin sideways, forearms flat and elbows bent, the weight of his upper body supported by the wood of the bar. Do you like boys? Wilhelm asked, his blond hair dripping rain, the bright foreign eyes dark in the pub's light.

Martin bypassed the scorn in his throat, covered it with a laugh, and said, I reckon in Oz they teach us to not ask after what's bloody obvious.

Wilhelm laughed. Same in my country, old man, he said. Same in my country. Only what I'm trying to say is that the truth isn't so obvious with you. Oz, eh? I've heard other Aussies call it that. What's behind the curtain—right, my friend?

Martin had already calculated that playing dumb in stressful travel circumstances was actually smart. Not knowing what was average conversation at a bar in America meant he didn't know if a reaction was called for in the bringing up of such a personal subject. He had mates. He liked his mates. So he stayed mute. He'd also come to understand he appealed to certain kind of men. He'd been approached several times al-

ready. Had no means to know what to do. Pops had not prepared him in this way. He doubted anyone in his family ever
gave thought to it. Sex was for making babies. It was practical.

The empty pints stacked; all bad feelings faded. Over the
range of a half-dozen nights at The Munich, Martin came to
like the rakish ways of Wilhelm and to appreciate the time
spent conversing about life philosophies, learning about bisex-
uality and homosexuality. When Martin decided after a few
weeks that New York hadn't the stuff to keep him and bought
an Ameri-Pass from the Greyhound bus line, he encouraged
Wilhem to consider travelling with him. It's not about liking
boys, Martin said. I've one sheila on my mind and nothing
else. But we make good communication partners. We might
have a few more stories to tell.

Wilhelm thanked Martin, said he wasn't done with New
York. And that was it.

Martin rode long into the American night and through a
day to Chicago, seated next to a mild-faced older woman who
encouraged him to talk around all the sides of his life so far,
which led him to marvel about why he felt so dejected when
Wilhelm hadn't want to travel with him. Which led to Martin
pulling out for the first time the jarrah box with the little knit
hospital cap and the photos in it. Led to him telling about his
mom, about Piotr, about how much he missed Pops, Annalesa,
Barney, and especially Jenny Kay. He told her about the seizures, and about what to do if he happened to have one.

When they parted ways the next morning, the woman
shook his hand and kissed his forehead, telling him everything
was going to work out right. Things happen as they need to
happen, she said, don't be in a hurry. Why, you're just a boy
yet in experience. A man in years, maybe, but you've got some
catching up to do.

Despite the discomfort of confinement and the odd natures
of footloose Americans, Martin found several things to like
about traveling about the United States on a bus. For one thing,

it gave him a chance to see the great nation as a series of freeze-frames. The effect was that of watching a motion picture, at times only the visual, no soundtrack, at times punctuated by the snorts and sneezes of fellow passengers and the murmur of transistor radios sizzling around the dial in search of local programming. Even further in the background, the gulp of the metal toilet back of the bus, the sting of cigarette smoke, the mixed smell of whiskey and Coca-Cola swirling together over cubed ice in truck-stop paper cups. The giggles of the sheilas as the lads poured it. The low-throat syllables of the lads urging the sheilas to sip. Deep in the night, one of the gals disappearing into the loo, followed by one of the lads, followed by the hushed rustle of clothing as the other passengers moved around, trying to pretend they didn't notice. The feigned silence as one by one the two returned to their seats.

He expected all of America to look like either the glitzy New York streets or a Clint Eastwood cowboy picture. What he didn't expect was the dark green of Pennsylvania and spotted milk cows of Ohio. That so much of the country was grassland surprised and disappointed him. Seemed it should all be tin baubles, neon, high-gauged traffic, sirens, and skyscrapers. He didn't expect pink dawns and knolls and cattle. He started thinking America was misrepresenting herself to the rest of the world.

Until the bus drove under the great arc of letters spelling the word *Chicago*, and the cityscape kicked in again, and Martin felt he was back in the cinema.

The bus driver downshifted his way from the highway to the central business district, the smell of gears and heated brakes strong enough to make people lower their windows. He talked into his microphone about keeping seated until the bus stopped, then yelled out, *Chica-a-a-go!* as passengers stood to gather wrinkled brown sacks of belongings, tripped over empty beverage bottles and cans, stretched and rummaged the overhead racks for what belonged to them. Yanks did not appear to be as tidy as Aussies or Brits. Martin had his knap-sack and small grip. The wait in Chicago was six hours, the bus sharing a terminal with the train station. The bloke next to him recommended paying to lock up his goods so he could go see the Sears Tower—the world's tallest building. According to the bloke, it was three bucks highly worth it. At the top, you could reward yourself with a *brewsky*, as he called it. Martin thought the idea amicable enough, paid his US quarters for a storage bin and key, made a quick tour of the station, finding nothing necessarily awful about it except for the panhandlers and loafers who started on him the minute he took the coin out of his pocket. The distraction muted his expectations and sur-prised him when he stepped into Chicago's silver combination of rain and sunshine.

New York had been uncommon. He wasn't a charmer with words like Pops, but he had a mind about land and the way it settled on a person. New York hummed and popped and was lit with light the way he expected, with the hopes and attitudes of her people. People came to New York full of wanting. You could feel that wanting in the air.

Chicago had the opposite sensation about it—a heart for whatever came, a preference for slow understanding. Various brochures Martin had run across made reference to America's Heartland. He understood how that sentiment arose. Chicago hit a bloke about the middle. Chicago was a poet's city, a feel-ing man's city.

Inside the Sears Tower the marble floor spread out in front of him looking slick as waxed parchment. People milled about with coats draped over their arms, school kiddies with their wee tourist sacks, blokes with cameras aimed to ceiling height, the scrolls and architectural features. Martin felt dumb as a bat. He bought his ticket and took the first lift, not certain it was the place he wanted to be. The car was full of sheilas and kids, all with the same giddy, holiday-free air about them. The mix caused Martin to feel rotten, knowing the kind of plush life they likely had, and here poor Jenny Kay was back in Gillagong, pouring the taps nightly and staying in the little room overhead so as to guarantee cheap living. *Spend not, want not,* she always said. She didn't even come to see him in hospital after his last seizure. Said it was a long road from Gillagong to Perth: better spare the petrol.

He came to with a constable standing over him holding ice to Martin's forehead. In the background the voice of a sheila saying she was a friend and would get him to medical care.

His next memory was of the sheila passing a biscuit, saying, *Eat. It's a bagel. Bread. Drink some juice.*

When he returned to the world it was dark, bus engine idling, the smell of fuel. The seat beside him vacant. Gears shifted to reverse, then neutral again, just as the abrupt sound of the undercarriage stowage doors lifting aroused the curiosity in everyone. This was followed by the long rake of cargo entering the bay, which caused a collective short breath to be held in wait of an explanation. The driver opened the door, and quick as that, Martin lost his spare seat. The night went from comfortable and stretched out to long and sleepless.

Then he remembered her. She was Stephanie Clark, and her bicycle would ride in a long, thin box she purchased from the ticket counter for five American dollars. She was biking across the United States but needed a break so was riding the bus from Chicago to Minneapolis. It was a lie when she had said she knew Martin well enough to know how to help him through one of his episodes. Crowds, she had told the copper, crowds bring it on. She told all this to the American police, then she walked Martin back from the Sears Tower.

The time spent and the dollars were worth it, standing up there, viewing the jagged, angular world of Chicago from above the skyline, until he stepped into the lift for the ride down from the top, and the cage began filling with mercury. He held to his souvenir bag with the tiny replica tower and the explanation leaflets with one hand, clawed against mercury with the other, trying to keep afloat. The crowd in the lift hushed, and he tried to explain what was happening so as not to scare them. Bloody mercury is what came out. Bloody mercury, he said, bleeding bloody mercury. Stephanie Clark stood beside him, caught his elbow like she knew he was going to fall, helped him to the floor. Somebody talked into the emergency phone. Somebody moved the crowd open for the coppers when the lift reached the ground floor, motioned to Stephanie, told them he was with her.

Once she got situated in the seat, she slipped him a stick of peppermint and told him to suck on it, said it would open back up his senses a bit, which it did.

* * *

It'd been a thirty-mile day in his inaugural week on a touring bike. Stephanie cranky and vocal about hoping he'd be able to cover more ground. He was trying to show her Baby Michael's gauze hospital cap and the Polaroids. She kept refusing to look at them.

God, Marty, she was saying. Sincerely. Should you be...? Is it healthy to be carrying those things around?

Crikey, Martin said. A man doesn't think about *healthy*. He thinks about what he needs at the time.

Well, Americans think about healthy, Stephanie said. *I* think about healthy. Look. Look, you just need fresh air and a change of diet. I think I'm here to help you get over this.

Stephanie dished up a campfire dish of eggplant and something she brought along in her kit called TVP, which came from soybeans, which Martin had never eaten. She did not eat meat and although Martin had never considered the like before, he had to admit he was feeling robust, making him glad for Stephanie's odd ideas about tucker. After the vendor fare at the bus terminals, bean cakes were at least a change of pace. Wrapped in plastic and labeled Pemmican, they were supposed to equal the potent sustenance needed by a cave-man. Martin liked them well and good enough, bought a sup-ply along with Stephanie at a market called Food Cooperative in Minneapolis, so far this week making brekky and tea of it.

We'll take a break from native food in Deadwood, Stepha-nie said, handing him a fig bar. Find a diner and eat eggs and grits. She handed him the cookie like it was Austrian crystal, or she was Austrian crystal. Martin thought she radiated light close up the way the bush radiated heat at a distance. He no-ticed it made his pulse tap with a certain tenderness. his willy throb for her woman parts. She read to him by firelight, a book called *Atlas Shrugged*.

We did book learning in Peabody School, Martin said. Spun a globe and saw an atlas, too. I saw America before I saw it, I reckon.

It was a hard book to catch listening, like William Shake-speare, but he listened as she read, every third night or so switching chores: Martin reading, she cooking; she cooking, Martin reading. He figured some of it to go in, but not much. He'd rather listen to music, he reckoned.

They got on, and they got on. Playing house from a tent. The smell of bicycle chains and rubber wearing off the tread, glue from patch kits. Kissing the bite away for each other from scraped skin when maniac *pickups*—as he learned to call them instead of *utes*—swerved toward them, spewing rock dust that ground against the enamel of their teeth. The smiles and hand-shakes of locals who let them camp on their lawn, shared pots of stew, poured whiskey shots.

I'm pregnant, she said one morning, a few months in, lying beside him, sleeping bags zipped together because it was cold, so their separate skin warmed neighboring skin and morn-ing sex came easily and lasted long, its rousing effects more dependable than the stoutest cup of coffee, the warmth ready and without the intolerable breach of mountain air waiting outside the tent flaps. They slept in the shadow of the Snowies near Havre, Montana, the range living up to its name with its brilliant white drifts reflecting light, stark and prominent. The image of those brilliant peaks blazed in Martin's brain as he scrambled for the tent zipper, the floor without warning turning to mercury, rising quickly to the height of his hips, his stomach, his neck, wobbly as Jell-O, until it filled his nose and plugged his breath.

He came to consciousness in a hospital bed in Havre, Montana, between white sheets, a tube running to a needle in his arm, his chest taped to wires running to a bleating machine, a note from Stephanie on the bedside: *I was only kidding!! I wanted to see what you'd say!!* Two exclamation points per sentence, Martin noticed, one for each bout of mercury she'd witnessed.

It was the Havre doctor who took time with him. His name was Seipel, German-glasses bloke with tired wheels at the side of his eyes and the promise of a paunch at his middle. He wore a lightweight suit coat but no tie. Funny attire, Martin thought, for a medico, accustomed as he was to the white coats of doctors, but Seipel's words held weight. Martin would buy into believing him if it'd throw a spanner in the mercury's appearances. He spoke in a wise, congenial way that made Martin think he'd better bring himself around to agreeing with his view. *Seizure* was the word he used over and over again. *Seizures.* And *seizure medication.* He asked if Martin had ever had absences, or situations where he'd go unconscious for a while. The chap also asked about other features of Martin's family, if any of them were crook. He gave Martin a supply of pills to take with him. No alcohol, he said. And no driving a vehicle.

Martin thanked the man and stood from the exam table, took the first pill and the little paper cup of water. At first they'll make you want to sleep, he said. But you'll get used to them, and any somnolent effects will wear off. It's not clear on the electroencephalograph that there is an electrical problem, but we can't verify it without a reading during an active event. If the medication helps, we know we're on the right track. But you need to stay close to a doctor. You'll need to be watched after.

About that time a nurse came in and handed over Martin's clothes. Martin threw the pills into the depths of his pack, walked the shiny floor past other nurses and said good day to all of them. They were wonderful, those nurses. Smart. Capable. Once outside Martin found his bike chained to a stair rail, assuming Stephanie had seen to it, strapped on his helmet, kicked up the kickstand. Up ahead was the light gray of the Montana day. By bike he couldn't make it to any town in any direction—Missoula or Kalispell and certainly not Thompson Falls—before night, but hopefully one of the bergs in between would have at least a diner where he could buy his tucker.

In the end Martin turned back and decided to stay in Havre that night, then a day later determined it might do him good to stay until the spring of the northern hemisphere year. He took a job washing dishes, getting paid under the table because of his travel visa. Weeks of taking the pills went by and no sign of the bloody mercury.

The thing about Havre that caught him up was cowboys. Of course he had been taught to call them waggies, an old-fashioned term of Pops' that no one in America seemed to have ever heard of.

The entire world knew about cowboys. He'd seen them often enough in the cinema. This was the America he was after. Mountains. Not the America of TV shows but the America of John Wayne and bloody Willie Nelson and *Bonanza*. This was the America of books and movies, the America of catalogs and magazines. The America that all this time had been pulling at him.

The West.

Of course, he had never envisioned himself washing bloody dishes, still at times woke from sleep to stare at the tent top wondering what he was doing. But then he put his feet out of his bivvy into the chill, unzipped the tent to see his bicycle leaning on a tree tall as a high-rise, smelling the plant life in the air, the green of it. *Chlorophyll.* Across the distance, white clouds with deep gray bottoms dropping rain on one tiny place in striped sheets called *squalls*. Martin had never seen its equal: in his part of Australia, if it worked up the guts to squall in one place, the whole bloody world was a squall.

Some mornings he woke to a brace of snow, flakes looking like shreds of tissue until they hit a hand, then vanishing as if they'd never been real at all. On his days off he hiked up the mountain to where snow was still stacked, pitched his tent in it. On cold mornings he liked to lie down and comb snow onto his chest until he could no longer stand the cold. Sometimes he lay too long, because he started getting the feeling he could just lay there and fall asleep. Cold and ice kills a bloke same as dry and heat. *Pale as mourning/the morn of my earth.* Words his mom helped him write for his poetry class at the Peabody District School and which always came to him when he was on his back like that, looking into the bonnie blue American sky.

He'd wanted to write death instead of earth, but his mother wouldn't hear of it. I can't bear to hear those words together, she said.

All that changed when one Sunday a pair of cowboy-sorts in a big American ute drove up to tell him he was on private property, that he had to sign on for work or vacate. He started to tell his story about Stephanie Clark ditching him, but before he could get a full sentence out, one of them said, Crawk-o-dial Dun-Day, eh? Hey, Willis! We got ourselves Crawk-o-dial Dun-Day. Ever wrestle a crawk-o-dial, Dun-Day? Hey, Willis! If he's wrestled crawk-o-dials, heifers oughtn't to be shit. What say, Crawk-o-dial? We got a brandin'. Best join before you freeze. Crawk-o-dial Dun-Day. Shit fire. Well, Mellon'll slap his own ass over this one, I predict.

Willis shifted to neutral, set the brake, and the conversational chap loaded Martin's bike and gear, motioning for Martin to climb aboard, too.

***

At first he abhorred the smell of hay, swatting cattle tails, and dust motes in hayloft sun. He came to appreciate the smell of a fork of barley and a bucket of oats in the morning for the devotion it brought him from the horse he was using—Hocus, they called him—even if he dreaded having to retrieve the animal from the horse barn where the rest of the *hands* (Hey, Asshole, it's hand, Willis said to Martin that first day. Not fucking waggy. These men are *hands*. Fucking brain dead asshole anyway) leaned their boots and talked amongst themselves. First they made fun of him because his roper boots were bloody new—*Get some shit on those boots, Crawk-o-dial*—they said, every day for a week. Then somebody hauled his bike on a sunny day onto a tack shed roof. When Martin questioned a few of the other cowhands to find out who, he got only shrugged shoulders and upturned palms, blokes adjusting their hats downward as if the sunlight were suddenly scarring their faces.

The white-haired bloke named Tippetts said Martin was the low hen in the hen house. You gotta understand, Tippetts said, you're a foreigner. I guess you could say some folks feel privileged on account of this place belongs to them.

Martin said, Not much on visitors, I reckon.

No, son, Tippetts said, not much on visitors. Not that we ain't ever had any. But the same hands come back year after year. This is our home and our livelihood for all of us. Family, some would call it. You was trespassing.

That was about as meaningful as conversation had gotten, otherwise it was hazing and jokes. Tedious. Although a time or two Martin couldn't help himself but flat laugh. Two cowhands put on like they were marrying each other after Martin told one bloke about Jenny Kay. The chap turned his singlet over his head similar to a sheila's wedding veil. Another filled a sock full of beans and let it hang out his buttons like it couldn't do its duty. Mellon saw, didn't comment, but the next day said to Martin, Some men come around to the life and some don't. But there's a ten-spot extra on your hire-on wages if you stick it out. You're a good hand. It's obvious you've been made to work. Let it roll off. End of the drive, go with 'em to town and buy a round. Hell, if what they want is *Crawk-o-dial Dun-Day*, give 'em it with bells on, you know? What is it you call—blokes? Hell, bloke 'em up. Call 'em every Aussie shit name in the book. The men ain't but bones and blood. Words is just words. You got just as many of 'em as they do.

Martin wanted to argue. Words were not just words. Words created the picture in his mind as a lad that made him dream of America. Every time Willis put on his phony Pom accent and said, *Harvey, ol' chap, I believe I've caught myself somethin' alien*, Martin would feel a dark sigh rise in his chest that failed to leave. It squashed his insides until there was a hollowness, same as he felt after his mom walked away. Same lunacy of hurt feelings.

Pardon me, have you any gray poop on? It was Willis again, leaning over the pommel of his saddle, lariat in hand, howling with laughter. They were preparing another branding for a herd of calves that had been born in barns and paddocks and belonged to ranchers downriver from the Milk River Ranch. They'd been driving them three days, most of them, along granite ridges and across spring melt drainages with north-facing drifts still taller than his head. It was like riding the bicycle for the first few days: the newness exhausted him. But instead of the whir of pedals and smell of bitumen against tires, it was the walking-stick movement of horse limbs, shanks shifting beneath him and the effort it took to fall into sway with the motion. His spine and pelvis pitched according to the rhythms of the landscape, the gold and sage and purplish shadows flowering from the jut of charcoal-colored outcroppings. The sky scraped the mountains into shapes distance erased, while his ass molded into a leather saddle and sunlight flashed in the silver stirrups and spurs of the other cowhands, whose starched silhouettes and sheepskin coats and neckerchiefs matched his; the white gauze of cold air from their combined breathing big as that of the steam valves at Perth's railyards.

Martin had in mind to undrape his quirt to see if he couldn't change the shape of Willis's nose. Instead, he watched him ride to the opposite side of the corral and cast his rope about the ankles of one of the larger calves. Most likely a single birth, since Mellon said singles are often bigger, or born early-season and therefore a mite older. Martin had at least learned enough to recognize the early-season from the late ones. He'd gotten much of his cowboy information from Mellon, who also loved to talk about local mountain history and the life of a rancher.

Mellon was a far cry better than Willis. Still, for all Willis's bad manners and lack of parlor manners, he was fine to watch in the roping pen. The rotation of his lasso was smooth and elegant, a bit of art. Pops would love that scene as he loved a job well done.

Willis's lariat spun and sang its miracle way around a pair of bucking calf's hooves. Quite poetic and a contrast considering it led to blood. Then he cinched it, pulling the rope taut with a halt and wave motion, backing his horse up, blokes and animals, flying into action—arms, leg, red-hot iron, scalpel, metal immunization gun. In seconds it was over, branding iron still pulsing with small waves of heat, the thick-throated sound of shock and disbelief from the calf—who not only got their hides seared with the ranch's brand, ears notched with a wide V, but their gonads sliced off and tossed into a pan, which everybody then ate. One of the older hands dredged them in flour and dropped them in hot fat. Then the little tiger was up and loose, relieved by freedom, acting at first as if nothing had happened, then dropping his head, embarrassed, ambling uncertainly toward the scream of his mother. Nose to nose, her nudges soothing his shame.

In the first month of employment with Mellon and the Milk

Ranch, Martin rode the hazing, which meant he herded calves away from their mothers, observing the first three brandings from atop his horse. At the fourth they gave him the vaccination guns, big silver metal plungers with tubes inside, two of them, one in each fist, his job to stab through the calf's tough hide.

Hazing cattle was a slightly boring job, made him pick up bad habits like dipping snuff and spitting tobacco juice at the dogs, as he'd watched Willis do. Just around the time of day he'd feel tired and hungry enough to wish for his swag, one of the cows would begin dodging and stomping at the herd dogs as if gone wacko over the notion of never getting back to her offspring, intent afterwards on running off by herself to bawl about her situation. Cattle weren't at all like roos, as when a joey wanders off, the mom doesn't give it a second thought. She moves on with her mob. By instinct she knows another joey will need her soon enough—roos season pretty often. If her joey doesn't come back on its own it starves, or gets hit by a motor vehicle, or, more's for certain, dies of dehydration.

At the end of the branding day, every set of dusty chaps hung on a hook, boots stashed at the base of bunkhouse beds, the smell of feet, whiskey, tobacco moving with the bit of breeze. Late at night, mouse work like the sound of crumbling crackers. Each night Martin could hear somebody with his head muffled by his pillow, bawling like those calves thrown down in the mud of the branding pen, separated from their mothers. He never did know who it was. The bloke cried those four nights and that was it.

***

Mellon decided to build a barn, which is what brought Martin to carpentering. Crazy, big, round pole-studded, open-rafter, finished-wall monster, which Mellon called the Pete French building after some early chap down in Oregon. Tippetts reminded Mellon before he started that nobody in Oregon liked Pete French, in fact somebody killed Pete French, shot him in the face. Mellon in response declared in front of all the hands at a Sunday afternoon barbecue to kick off the project that he didn't believe in superstition or hexes.

I am, he said, by God, gonna have myself a big, round barn like French's so I can winter cattle with mown feed and in style instead of my expensive herds freezing their asses off in the feedlot.

Martin couldn't imagine what kind of a giant of a barn he was talking about to house two thousand head, until Mellon showed the plans, all drawn out by an architect. A series of concentric inner and outer stalls in ramped, wedding-cake layers and shed partitions allowed for the dropping of bales onto one of the chutes running to the various layers right from the upper lofts for somebody else to fork it onto a rotating trough, just like that.

Are you sure you ain't talking about horses? Willis asked, slanting his hat back and scratching his forehead. Because it looks to me like you're talking an awful lot of alfalfa, and there ain't been a winter of any year in Montana got cold enough you couldn't drop a bale of hay into a meadow and a cow not have a notion to walk over and eat it. Now horses, I could part see it but not two thousand in one place. Smell alone'd be enough to make it hard to come to work in the morning, even for me. Whadya gonna do with the shit, boss man? You calculated that?

The shit will get hosed down a drain. Everyday. It'll be trucked off and sold. I've already got a buyer. Organic fertilizer. Marble fat is what I'm talking about, Mellon said. Black angus and marble fat.

Marble fat comes from feeding corn at the last, son. No news in that.

What cow did you ever know of who would march into a corn field to start shucking ears? It ain't natural for a cow to eat corn. I've been studying it. Meat with natural fat goes for a much higher price. Fewer head, less upkeep. More efficient.

Natural fat, Willis said.

That's what I said. Natural fat. I aim to do an experiment. I want to prime and fatten at a natural rate on the hoof. We'll do more wide-ranging. We'll have to do that. I'm also gonna buy Wagyus from Japan. They're all about marble fat. I'm gonna cross them with an angus. See what I get. See if I can make it pay for itself at the very least.

What the hell is a Wagyu? Sounds like a genital disease.

I've read about them, Mellon said. Only a handful in the United States right now. One guy brought some over back in '75. The meat is supposed to be like no other. Succulent, it's billed. Can you imagine the price you can put on succulent? Top dollar coming and going. You keep them inside of a winter at night, feed alfalfa and oats and keep 'em warm so they don't burn up their marbling like winter herds do just trying to keep from freezing to death. You ever think about that? That's money burning. I'm gonna build corrals and pens, make me a stack of dollar bills this ranch ain't ever seen. Then I'm gonna sell the whole blamed operation to you, Willis, because I'm getting close to being tired of it.

All the hands, including Martin, leaned on corral rails, listening. Willis raised his hand to Mellon's forehead like a mom checking a lad for fever. Either Mellon mistook the gesture or took it as a reason, because he clipped Willis's hand with an uppercut to the chin and a left to Willis's abdomen, doubling the man over square in the middle like a sack of peanuts. Martin thought it funny, watching these things happen just like the movies. Nobody said a word or moved or made any sound. Willis picked himself up, slapped his hat against the side of his pants to shift off the dust, rolled the inside of his hat crown against his fingers as if searching for the middle of it before putting it back on his head. Wonder where that's coming from, he heard somebody whisper, which started the murmuring.

Back in the bunkhouse that night, everybody said the same thing. Something had come over Mellon lately, and he was taking it out on Willis. A few thought the argument was over Mellon's wife, or one of his daughters. Nobody could really say. None of them had ever met Mellon's family, only spotted them getting in and out of a truck or the big, black sedan Mellon drove into town on the weekends. He kept his women far back from the work and the men, except for Willis and Tippetts. Some mused that Willis tried to lay one of the daughters who was said to have been in a Hollywood film. Martin could have offered his opinion but held it back. He'd seen Pops go on lunatic building sprees often enough to know if Mellon was high on the idea of a new barn, something was making him sore in the tooth.

Right away the barn got started. Willis lined up the men to draw from a tobacco can slips of paper with tasks described on them. Martin got the chore of building footing frames while others started excavating. One bloke down on his hands and knees trying to hammer a boulder into pieces took a sliver of granite to the eye and came back from the doctor with gauze and a black patch. The others spent a week calling him Popeye and Yosemite Sam and other references that meant fairly little to Martin. As Mellon had instructed, Martin swallowed hard and added to the teasing—this time by telling them that back home around Jelico, somebody'd call the bloke *tough on his missus*. The men looked confused until Martin felled the punch line: tripping over a stiffy in the a.m. and landing on the bedpost is the main way a bloke gets an injury like that.

All got quiet until his meaning trickled in, then chaps laughed and patted him on the shoulder, saying, Good one, *Dun-Day*. Chaffee, the mess cook, came around with a stack of foam cups and coffee. Mellon wanted to know who the hell gave call to start a party. The cook told Martin's joke, to which Mellon said, Have at it.

The date on Martin's wristwatch was April 28, one year

to the day since Willis and Mellon carted him off the Judith Mountains.

The carpentering took his mind away from the cold shadow of the Judiths and back to the heat of Jelico and Gillagong. It wasn't the frame he was pounding, but the boards of the cross Nate Cleary and the gang put up after the nail situation. It wasn't beams or rafters but the Outbound's decks, gathering building, the playground. The cold storage he and Jenny Kay built inside the Tanzey-Davis. How far he was from home. Whether it was bloody good or not, Martin couldn't tell. He had begun to feel smarter than most of the blokes on the ranch, recognizing none of them was genuinely what he would call *mates*. Now that he had reached the level of their match, he was starting to think about moving on. With each pound of the hammer, with each sheet-metal flange and stall frame he hung, he felt the spinning wheels of his bicycle. The barn might be done by June. If Mellon did what he said he was going to do insofar as tagging the dogeys and not immunizing—there wouldn't be any brandings.

As everybody put it, Mellon had gone soft in the heart.

So Martin started to envision a plan for loading his tent in his panniers and pedaling to Boise. He didn't know much about Idaho, but that's where Stephanie Clark had been heading. A person could only go so long in America without facing the citizenship question. If she were indeed pregnant, that would be his sign to make a choice about remaining.

He was up in the barn loft hammering the sheet-metal flanges that would work as a sort of aperture to deflect rain while still allowing a certain amount of sunlight into the barn's central corral. Nobody knew what Mellon's purpose was in this. Somebody said it looked like the inside of a chip burner. Since neither Willis nor Tippetts were arguing with Mellon anymore, nobody else was, either. The other men did as they were told and followed the architect's renderings.

Different this time. Those were the words that came mind

as the loft began filling with platinum-colored Jell-O: no unpleasantness. Martin watched it coming as if from way below, from the bottom of the round hay corral where other hands were pounding in plank flooring.

He began feeling tired in the eyes, the way he had that first week atop Hocus, nodding as the horse lumbered like a train car in its rocking, jarring rhythm. He lay down his hammer to rub the tiredness, but the level of the mercury instantly had reached his face. He did not fight, rather lay over on the scaffolding, which vanished along with him inside the mercury's hollow bubble.

When a man falls thirty feet from a scaffolding to a yellow poplar barn floor, one of three things happens. He breaks every bone on the side of his body and face he lands on. If it's his left side, he also ruptures his spleen. Or, the momentum causes him to break through the quarter-sawn planks, in which case he'll either land crossways of the floor joists and really do some damage, or parallel, if he's lucky, suffering a bit of bruising but otherwise just mashed up. No permanent damage with the latter. What happened in this case was that just as Martin leaned over the scaffolding, a skinny, brown-haired kid named Wyeth, nephew to Willis, stepped into the open space underneath. Martin hit him long ways, fracturing the kid's left collarbone and shoulder blade. The other hands working alongside him later said the barn's round shape made an echo like the sound of a gunshot against a canyon wall.

He came around this time in the back seat of Mellon's big, black sedan with Mellon driving, Willis riding shotgun—a phrase Martin had learned since coming to work on the Milk. He was a world of hurts—hurt to breathe, hurt to smell, hurt to feel the astringent taste in the back of his mouth he thought must have been his lunch upturned. Something on him must be bleeding, because his chest was wet, and there was the copper smell of butchering. He was back to feeling like he did in snow, the cold cramping his chest like a harness. Then, strange, Jenny

Kay held his head in her lap. She was wearing big shades, her hair in a bun. Martin thought it must be denim on her legs for the way the fabric felt against the nape of his neck and the way it smelled. Hey, Wes, I think your cowboy here's awake, the voice said in a rake-throated way that wasn't Jenny Kay's.

What say, Clarene? Mellon's voice. The tires on the car, the black rubber vaguely being sanded away. Martin heard the flow of the center line, the fog stripe. The Drury Road had neither. He dreamed of a pair of yellow stripes down the center of a road he could taste but could not see.

Later, in the fog, chlorine, squeaking noises moving at the pace of footsteps. The words spleen, lung, seizures. Dr. Seipel. A name spoken over the intercom to which Martin opened his eyes. A man in white coat and bow tie at the door conversing with Mellon and Willis. Next to those two towering men, he felt small as a lad in primary school and timid as one calculating the distance for a spit wad, whether he had time to load the straw and catapult the chewed paper before the teacher noticed. Muted roaring in Martin's head. Ears stuffed. He was back to the days of the terrible fever and the urge to yell, *Pinker! Pinker!* Did he speak? Dr. Seipel, Mellon, and Willis turned to him, as did the woman in the chair with the big sunglasses pushed atop her head.

Dr. Seipel, 331. Dr. Seipel, 331, the voice spoke from overhead. Dr. Seipel flashing a small light at Martin's eye and saying, Marty? Marty? Can you hear me? Can you tell me what day it is? Speak up, son.

***

Mellon's first reaction was to end Martin's employment at the MR Ranch, came into his hospital room speaking in legal terms. Words like litigation and lawsuit and torts. Things had ruptured—Martin's spleen and ribs, a lung, his skull suffering a fracture. He had *severe bilateral testicular contusion* and might never be able to be a dad at all now. His spleen rupture had caused *significant exsanguination into the abdominal cavity* and was *removed by laparotomy*. Martin had to be transfused. Dr. Seipel's words flew at him like shooting stars.

As to the balance of your injuries, Dr. Seipel said, The cerebral fracture was significant in that there was some *contre-coup effect* severe enough to cause nausea and vomiting, which was *being treated and appeared transient. Sequelae such as a coma would have presented by now.* The *pneumothorax resolved with treatment.* He paused to consult papers while Martin imagined himself as a collection of words from a textbook. Did the good doctor truly expect anyone to interpret what he had said, much less a man frizz-brained from medicine and injury?

Mellon's quick thinking and medic expertise in Vietnam saved Martin on that last one, Dr. Seipel said. The old ballpoint pen and clear wrap trick. In short, you're a train wreck, Mr. Tuor, but I've treated bull riders with worse. The more important question is whether you're taking your Dilantin, and if so, why were you thirty feet in the air on a plywood scaffolding? The sun probably created a strobe. What did you mean not telling your employer you have a seizure disorder? I've known Wes and Clarene Mellon half a century, delivered the girls, treated everything from a nail through the hand to chicken pox and tonsillitis. Mr. Mellon is screaming, and rightly so. Mr. Tuor, you can't have seizure disorder and not tell people. It's illegal for you to drive. You oughtn't be operating machinery. There's certain habits you have to break. But more than that, as I now understand it, you had the seizure *while* you were on Dilantin, correct? You took it as scheduled, never missed a dose, eschewed alcohol, is that correct?

Dr. Seipel's lecture had gone on so long, Martin thought he had dozed back off, but the silence stirred him. Never missed a dose, no sir, no I did not, Martin said. Something in the way the pillow held his head at just the right angle and the fluorescent lights being off and the door closed on the rest of the world and the tragedies people were making made him drowsy as the sea breeze coming into the gulf at Perth, the salt of it drifting so far it reached along the Outbound's dust lane to Martin, swinging in Pap's hammock, to the sound of kid voices—Nate-mate, Piotr, Annalesa. Martin swinging and swinging, nothing to do with the afternoon but fall asleep.

The hospital grapevine at Havre Memorial had it that Dr. Seipel could get himself investigated for talking to non-relatives about Martin's condition. That was what the ombudsman said when he came around to visit. Martin found himself asking about a raft of things he'd been wondering about since he came to America, like how does a chap get a social security card that Mellon at first said he needed and then said he could do without—they were used to paying blokes *under the table.* The ombudsman, an older chap, looked at Martin like he was daft when he said that, taking his pen out and making notes. The bloke was real nice, and after his visit Mellon gave him his job back—with a few conditions, such as Martin keeping his feet on the ground.

Once Martin was out of danger, Dr. Seipel released him from in-hospital and told him Mellon had paid the bill. Martin thought he'd miss these kind people who had taken such care of him, so told them to distribute the many flowers he'd received among themselves. A nurse kissed him on the cheek then called the only taxi in Havre, wheeled him out in a wheelchair. It was a beater of a ute, a white Chevrolet sedan with black letters along the door that read HAVRE CAB.

Fancy a smoke, mate? The driver had gotten out to help Martin into the front seat. He inched him along, as if practiced in helping the wounded move from one place to another.

Truth! You're from Oz, mate? Martin asked.

Down Coober Pedy. You, mate?

Bloody hell! Denton and Jelico. Bush side of Perth. Married a sheila out of Gillagong. Well, a US of A sheila transplanted to

Gillagong, but good enough. Crikey!

Goodonya. Not many of us out there now, is there? the cabby said, as he shook Martin's hand.

Nope. Nope, Martin said, but awe-inspirin' luck, isn't it? Just clear awe-inspirin' luck. Bloody hell. What a country. One minute you're loping alongside Yanks and their dogeys, next you're flat on your back in an infirmary with pretty lasses all concerned, leaning their norks in your face. Next thing you're running into a fellow bloody countryman.

Too right, the cab driver said. What puts you way out here, mate? He smelled of cigarettes and petrol.

A dark nurse's assistant brought out a sack of Martin's hospital belongings and pillows and blankets. She wore a beaded amulet Martin had come to recognize as meaning she was an American Indian. Similar to blackfellas in Australia. People who came first. She propped him with the pillows and fluffed a blanket over him. Cary here will bring it back, she said.

Crikey. Near broke the entire insides of myself, and for good, Martin said.

Once inside the ute, he was a blur from the middle out, where the cold outdoor air had originally revived him. It was a secondary feeling, as if some foreign agent were sending vibrations from his gullet to his noggin. He wanted to smack his skull to stop the waves, to keep them from carrying off his essential self, but he lacked energy. He settled in, nodded off before he could put his next question to the driver: what's the fee to Boise?

In the cab he dreamed of a graveyard where was buried the Queen Mother, his brother Piotr, Baby Michael, and a huge black hand. He'd been given a drug which provided him X-ray vision, meaning he could see beneath the settled layers of earth covering the contents of each grave. He could see the heft and weave of the burial clothes, the details of the skin, faces, even the eyelashes. No coffins, only bodies intruding into otherwise undisturbed ground. Martin stood over each, absorbing the particulars—the Queen Mother with her rubies and an old-style starched filigree neckline, diamond tiara, and matching earbobs; his brother Piotr, who was actually wide awake, startled Martin with a wave and a flashed grin; Michael, wearing his white knit hospital hat, clutching two Polaroids. In one, Michael was his infant self, perched atop a tiny bicycle inside his hospital incubator. In the other, he was partially decomposed with a filthy nappy tied across his head so that only the space where his little button nose should have been was exposed. Martin tried to lean closer, to see into Michael's brain pan in the second Polaroid, but the clapping began. He walked to the fourth grave to where the big, black hand was moving against its invisible other, the sound loud as thunder coming from directly overhead and within the hand's grave at once. But Piotr and the Queen Mother aren't dead, Martin said, waking himself.

They were waiting for him at a place called The Outrider in Havre. Mellon. Willis. The lot. Balloons and ribbons waving like a festival. The Pete French barn was nearly finished, they said, the herds at high elevations for summer grazing, the cowboys with seniority staying with the drive, the lesser ones still hammering or riding fence. For all the threats and ranting, Martin's position in the ranks seemed to have been saved, although one bloke Martin had never talked to before did tip his hat low and muttered words of which only *titty baby* and *boss man's marbles* were completely audible. Of course, Martin calculated Mellon's wife had something to do with this overall change of atmosphere, Mellon himself plonked and clapping Martin on his sore back. He refused what they poured him at first, ended up drinking anyway, despite Dr. Seipel's admonitions. One last time and then never again, he told himself.

Next morning he awoke in his old bunk, with a chunkering head and a picture of the night mixed in: Willis and Mellon daring him to climb onto the bar, saying, Give us a dance, *Crawk*-o-dial! The barkeep lasting Martin's wounds with a pair of towels and duct tape, the jelly-bottomed sheila named Winsom who climbed on with him, facing him, tables banging, whooping and hollering as she bucked his thigh while he pulled off her shirt, her bra, and she drove her tongue into his throat. He remembered her arching back and him sucking at her breasts, him rearing and unbuttoning his knickers up to the point the proprietor came racing over to pull the light cord over the bar from the power point, the crowd rejecting his actions with a roar, fists slammed, tables kicked over, beer mugs crashing, shattering, the smell of spilled beverage rising.

Martin couldn't recall much after that. Thought he must have popped a cluster of pain killers before climbing atop the bar. Thought it might have been the coppers pulled him off. He didn't know. Now here was Willis, leaning over him with a basin, a cold rag, and a pot of coffee. Martin took one sip of the latter, heaved it into the former, fell back on his pillow to cover his face with the one in the middle. He worried the mercury might show up, but it didn't.

The second time Willis came around, he carried a bowl of bouillon and a quart of orange juice. From the missus, he said, set them on the floor by the bunk and departed. The generous behavior was odd enough that Martin started spinning a story in his brain of how Winsom was Willis's secret girl, how Willis got jealous and jumped Martin, how the other blokes pulled him off because Martin was such a chap and bonny to have around. How in the melee Willis fell and hit his head and was now returning from his dark end to make amends.

Around sundown Willis came to the bunkhouse again, this time with a plate of beef and potatoes and cucumbers, all of which seemed real enough. Get it down if you can, Willis said, his shirt changed from workday denim to a white short-sleeved with a black bolo tie and silver conch. Spirits didn't change clothes. Weekend in Missoula, Willis said.

Martin let his legs over the side of the bunk onto the floor. The wood planks warm from the afternoon sun. Bloody turps, he said. Pops always told me never to touch the turps. Knew his business, I reckon.

Willis laughed and held out a bottle and a pair of tumblers. What say, Dun-day? Hair of the dog? Best cure for whiskey hangover is more whiskey.

Aye, Martin said, reaching to take the shot. Fair dinkum.

Willis rotated his hat as if wondering whether to speak.

Any idea...Martin started to say, but Willis interrupted.

As we say here, never look a gift horse in the teeth, you know.

I reckon, Martin said.

Fair dinkum, Willis said, and after a pause: Did I say it right?

Martin laughed. Aye, he said, I reckon so.

If Havre had been a mite larger, if he couldn't feel the pull of Stephanie Clark from all the way in Boise, and if he hadn't spent the summer healing and wondering if there'd been any truth to her pregnancy story, Martin might have stayed on with the Milk River Ranch bunch. By autumn, when they were starting to drive herds down from the mountains to the spanking new Pete French barn for that first winter experiment, Martin felt a twang of regret, missed the tick of a leather saddle under his ass. He thought he'd miss clearing out a season's debris, then rolling out his swag on a high-elevation cow camp bunk for the night or two they were lucky enough to be near one, where normally they'd ride part of the way back down the mountains to the big wall tents. He'd miss the secure feeling of a lump of jerky in his pocket, a kerchief to breathe into when the atmosphere got too cold, the heat of a fire at night and the promise of whatever the designated cook was stirring in the big cast iron pot or roasting underground in the Dutch oven. Martin was well aware he'd let himself be absorbed into this life, but he was also aware of the one out there waiting. The one he came to America for. In the last days of August, when he no longer had an excuse for lazing in the bunk, he sat on the porch with his boots on the rail, remembering himself as a kid, pasted by the nose to pictures and words and maps about the United States. He didn't want to go through his life muted by ignorance. He wanted what his body was compelling him to find out. He could feel himself pulled in this new direction as sure as if a lariat had him around the middle. He might be crazy as Piotr, but even if it were death itself tugging, he had no choice but to greet it. No matter how he turned the ball, time in the Judiths was over. Time on the Milk was over. Martin packed his grip, looked about the bunk to chalk it onto his memory, walked to the big house and shook hands with Mellon, hugged Clarene

Is Willis about? Martin asked, trying to pretend they weren't all staring at his packed grip and bicycle. If he is, would you let him go in the middle of the day? Long enough for a ride to the bus station?

***

Winchester, Idaho. Pearl of a town. A bloke only had to walk a short pace to refresh his feet in the water or plop down a few quid for his tucker. *A mo-bile home.* Crikey, it got hot inside that thing in the summer, until he found himself a used swamp cooler over in Lewiston at Steve's Pawn. Not quite as efficient as an air-conditioning unit, but good enough.

No sheilas to get tangled with in this part of the wood. Unless he counted gruff old grams and logger widows with tressed hair and glued fingernails. Logger widows only for nine seasons of the year, then those blokes were home and passionate about reclaiming their stakes for the winter. Friday nights at Grinch's during that time were a danger. Outside road train drivers and cane cutters, Martin had never seen men with arm girth to surpass those Winchester loggers. Or more emboldened by a tinnie. Milt at Buttress Hardware claimed he couldn't keep flannels in forty-four to forty-eight chest American. Forty-eight! When he was in rehab after his accident, Martin was a thirty-eight. Forty now that he was back working.

He'd likely never have discovered Winchester on his own, isolated in the mountains the way it was, kilometers from nothing, but after a frustrating time in Boise trying to track Stephanie Clark, he met a bloke during the bus ride lunch stop as he was headed back north to explore a town called Lewiston. Named John Glenn, the man was on his way to Winchester to operate a clinic.

Same as the astronaut, but no relation, John Glenn said.

Martin had been preparing to take his noon meal when John Glenn strolled in to purchase a sandwich and struck up conversation, Martin explaining that he had taken the Greyhound bus lines north again because—for one—he couldn't find a human in Boise who had ever heard of Stephanie Clark. Not in the telephone directory, not the information operators. Not the coppers. Not the hospitals where he thought she might've had to go to have a baby.

For two, he had heard that in Riggins he might get paid to oar whitewater for the end of the season. If that didn't work, then to Lewiston, which was said to be between two rivers and in a housing boom. Pounding nails got you paid under the table, John Glenn told him, and was the opposite of a quick ticket to the US Department of Immigration. Of course, Martin's body was still banged up a bit at that point, but he expected himself to be mended enough to pull oars, at which he no experience, but had a mind to learn, or swing a hammer. He had a supply of medicines for lingering aches and pain, plus some to stop him from having another seizure. When Martin discovered this John Glenn was a medico and told him his story, the bloke perked right up, said he had treatments that might help further, suggesting Martin be his first patient in this new town.

I worked on a Harvard study, the man said. The point was to distinguish the relationship between seizures and hallucinations.

In that instant Martin felt skeptical, but the chap's enthusiasm toward the subject of Winchester and Martin's history was infectious, so he decided to invest a bit of time, climbing into John Glenn's ute instead of renting a room in Riggins as he had planned.

Next thing Martin knew, two weeks had passed, and he was signing his name to lease a caravan in the city of Winchester, right smack off the central business district on a bubbly patch of bitumen known as Morning Glory Acres.

At first it had been all right. Still he wondered whether he had been off his noggin to begin with to come all the way from Western Australia just to settle in some bloody mountain village in Idaho. It certainly was not a life he had ever thought of for himself. Back in Peabody District School as a kid, he pictured himself a grown man standing in front of a classroom spouting dates to school kiddies and stories about distant places. In those days he wanted to know every dot on the map. When the Cleary boys told him books would turn him into a poofter, and his Pops confirmed it, that was the end of that.

Just past eight a.m., he and John Glenn rolled into Winchester that first day. The bloke was a top-of-the-morning-to-you early riser, pounding on Martin's motel door at five. Rise and set with the sun, he had said, and you'll heal ills you don't know you have—sounding a bit like Pops.

Martin had not gotten used to the world reversed, which is to say, the north of North America having extended daylight hours during the time of year he grew up calling winter. Nonetheless, there the chap was, standing at the door with his cowboy vest, pearl-snap shirt, and pointy boots, just like the hands at the Milk Ranch had worn for going to town, only he could smell the new on John Glenn's from a social distance, namely the giveaway odor of cheap leather. The clothes matched his longish sideburns and strong aftershave in a Saturday-night-with-a-sheila sort of way.

Winchester's first impression made Martin want to remember the date, August 4, which happened also to be his sister Annalesa's birthday. How old was she now? Thirty-three? Thirty-five? He had thought the town of Winchester a beaut equal to a sheila. You wound up to her from the main highway through groves of conifer and aspen along a drop-off. It was good road but loopy as an egg-warm snake. If Americans drove on the left the way they did back home, he'd have been worried about the wheels of John Glenn's Trooper dropping into the mist. As it went, they drove the bank side, which transformed pretty quickly into a straightaway ending at the top of the hill at the red stop sign. The T-intersection created a corner for a signboard big as a building that read, *Annual Winchester Rodeo Days. Third Weekend in August. Second Oldest Rodeo in the West.*

Kitty-cornered was a glass-front café. Likely the source of the meat-frying smell which had begun seeping in and around the ute's window edges.

Oh yes, John Glenn said, cranking the wheel left and looking at Martin, who couldn't help but stare at his own eyes and nose bulging in the man's reflective lenses.

Chicken gizzards. Best anywhere, he continued, pulling in front of the building, the name Old-Time Café painted on its windows. A stylish, heavy woman with brightly-colored jewelry was lowering an awning, the stripes of which were red and white as Christmas lollies.

Chooks, Martin said. Where I come from we call them chooks.

John Glenn went on to calculate aloud whether the frying and the size of the woman's hips were connected. Martin had noticed women in Montana and Idaho carried more weight than women in other places in the US. The cold, dark winters, he reckoned. Women in Western Australia tended to be lean. In the bush they burned it off working from dawn to night. Town women walked all over. Nobody started an auto to drive fewer than a couple of miles. People used transport, too, which meant walking or riding a bike to loading shelters. In Winchester it wasn't just the sheilas. His first glimpse inside Old-Time Café proved that. Sitting at the counter were a half-dozen men with bellies round and full enough to house a joey, framed by galluses. Another meaty chap in motorcycle getup sat by the front window rubbing the bugs from his helmet faceguard with napkins he dipped in his water glass. That was another thing: a glass of water handed out in every diner. In Oz they drank beer. Maybe that was the case after all. Maybe Aussies were lean because beer kept them pissing it out.

Best gizzards any place, John Glenn repeated, slipping into the booth while leaving Martin the chair. They don't skimp. All you can eat. Three dollars plus potatoes and salad. Take it to the tavern to eat with beer, if you want to. I like the environment here better.

The waitress who had unfurled the awning put a pair of menus atop their plates and nodded her head once her in their direction. Gents, she had said. My name's Arlette, and I'm happy to report I'll be your waitress. Special is Ham 'n' Easy, three-ninety-eight.

She looked tired but like she was having fun. It was the slight sag of her jowl and the sad little nose, which appeared side-swiped, the left nostril shriveled compared to the right. Yet she had huge eyes, full of a hint of mischief, with faint cosmetics. Her morning lipstick now just a smear around the edges of her mouth. Martin felt an urge to comfort her, could see far enough into the future to know for a fact that one day he'd step into the Old-Time Café to sit at the counter when no one else was there and that he and she would exchange stories. John Glenn ordered gizzards for Martin, insisting he try them. The mere thought of eating such an animal part repulsed Martin. Still, his mom had taught him never to be rude to a host, so instead of complaining or arguing, he walked to the next counter where Arlette was chatting with her regulars to order a glass of orange juice, hoping to balance the nutritional deficit.

Of course, Honey, she said, then tipped the pitcher wrong and spilled juice across the counter, which led to her picking up and cleaning under half-eaten plates of food while fending off her patrons wise-mouthed comments.

***

Winter came hard to the mountains of North Central Idaho that first year.

He had thought Montana was bad enough, working in the Judiths. Montana cold cut right through layers of wool flannel. Nothing helped but a sheepskin topper, which was mildly funny, coming clear from Western Australia and a childhood revolving around a reformed sheep station to shiver inside a sheepskin topper. Shearers stopping at the Tanzey-Davis in Gillagong used to joke about how they'd rather skin a ewe than keep clipping them time and again, especially the willful ones. Martin interjected once to point out how many blokes wore sheepskin coats compared to how many people in general wore wool toppers or sweaters or slept under wool rugs. The sweaty, dirt-caked mob of shearers gawked until Martin shrugged and tipped his beer their direction, at which point most of the blokes laughed and somebody asked how he managed to rummage tucker for himself. Jenny Kay had stepped in and gonged her great brass bell, and the chaps turned back in on their own circle. It took a while, but it finally hit Martin that they didn't want to skin ewes. They were simply fine with having the subject in common.

Plus, winter in Montana came with bloody bales of hay to be reckoned with, equal to a road-train load, to be lifted off the ground and pitched on a trailer bed: *bucked* the Yanks called it. Two thousand head to be fed, winter from October to May. That first season he wore through the fingers on three pair of leather work gloves. The sheepskin topper he bought from a catalog after Mellon pulled him aside and told him his bargain-store wool wouldn't do for shit.

Even though the snow along the Milk itself had reached thigh-deep and to fifteen feet higher in the Judiths, and the wind dragged the temperature down to thirty below in Fahrenheit, the Winchester winter of 1990 made his two winters in Montana look like a greeting card. Snow even down the mountain in Lewiston, two feet deep on New Year's Eve, and it situated at near sea level. The foothill towns ascending into the Bitteroots and Northern Rockies were in mayhem. One street plow for Winchester, Craigmont, and Nez Perce. People had their snow shovels out, clearing the streets by hand. The Old-Time and Grinch's provided coffee and pastries. Buttress Hardware sold hats and mufflers and mittens at a discount. A couple of blokes from Waha with snow blades hooked to their one-tons showed up to finish the job. Everybody told weather stories, including Martin, who told about the year of the Wednesday Flood. People mostly took the interruption to their routines good-naturedly. John Glenn afterwards offered spinal alignments for half price. The townsfolk had by that time gotten used to his methods, as had Martin: the man's plasters and herbs healed for some folks in a few weeks what months and years of current-day medicine hadn't been able to do.

What the bad weather meant for Martin was, of course, no construction jobs, until John Glenn decided he wanted cabinetry in his office, offering to buy the necessary tools. The bloke insisted his cabinets be built the old way, with hand-carved dowels, dovetails, shellac from actual beetle shells. It was the carving that Martin enjoyed the best. He worked in the evening on a small, flat box decorated with flowering vines to replace the jarrah one that had housed his dead son's nursery cap. By the time he'd finished and took it in to show Arlette at the Old-

Time, word about his carving and woodworking skills started getting around to where soon he had a stack of orders ranging from rosette drawer pulls for Gypsy Feingold's wife, Yara, to a humidor carved with a Celtic cross for Tom at the post office.

***

In the background he studied for citizenship, sitting on his front steps reading and jotting notes about American history and events—and not turning into a poofter after all. Finding enough satisfaction in woodworking to keep him in American dollars. Craving the letters from his sister Annalesa telling him about their older brother Piotr's trips for electric treatments. Stories from Barney's struggles at uni, trying to decide what he should become. Pops pining away his later years over Mom, the way it magnified the pain of aging for him. The calendar rolled and rolled until the day came in July, 1992, a day he felt he somehow had been waiting for. He was inside the shed he'd insulated and wired, when a song came to him, a song his mom used to sing when he was a kid frustrated over learning to tie his shoes or the alphabet or his sums, a song he hadn't thought of in years. The sound of his voice and work muffled by a summer rainstorm hitting the windows: *Be patient, be patient/don't be in such a hurry/Be patient, be patient/you'll only start to worry…*

An image of her clear and astonishing as if she were beside him filled his heart and body, big as the room. He sat on a wood stool at the end of his work table as tears dripped onto the sawdust. It didn't take a medico to diagnose it. He knew well as he knew his own name that the mom he hadn't seen in more than twenty years had died.

Martin walked to John Glenn's house behind his offices to tell him about it because he couldn't stop crying. He was near convulsing from it. I don't keep sedatives, of course, but this will help, John said, as he opened a bottle of wine and pulled from his pocket a Baggie of something white, one of something green, and another of what looked like dried mushrooms, gray-brown. Came to me today in the way of payment for services, he said. I don't ordinarily do this kind of thing, but I have, and I had a feeling it might come in handy. Now it has. This one will make you brave, he said, pointing to the white one. Pointing first at the green one, then the brown, he said, This one will open your mind. This one will open your eyes.

I don't engage with such things, mate, Martin said, shocked to his core.

My friend, change is the solitary dependable characteristic of life, John said. The man reminded Martin of Pops musing about the value of white coats and the syringes of medicine used to quiet his brother Piotr.

Martin knew at its commencement it was a journey for which he never should have taken the first step. He'd never before that night sucked any substance up his nose besides bathwater. A bean one time, for which Pops fetched Dr. Warren/Wallaby. The potions lay in front of him like sorcery. He remembered a talk with Stephanie Clark over the enhancing qualities of marijuana. She always lit up before sex. He had not for one minute wondered how it would be. Now he *was* wondering. He wanted the pain of what he understood was the loss of his mom—for the second and more permanent time—to be gone, even if just for a short moment so he could catch his breath. John Glenn must have glimpsed his curiosity, because he took out a pinch of the white powder, humped it in a little line on the table, demonstrated the process for taking it in, which involved a nostril held closed.

The effect on Martin's mind and aching heart after he tried a limp sniff at the stuff was one of quick and immediate brightening, as if heaven itself had entered his skull and turned up the wattage. The metallic taste at the back of his throat was equally bright. Bright and brassy. John Glenn talked on and on, but Martin didn't care and didn't hear much of what he said from that point on. He was too busy suddenly understanding how aware he was of the space between the raindrops trailing down the windows.

***

After that night, strange events started happening. He started finding items that didn't belong to him. Belongings were missing. Bastards let themselves in his house when he was out. Crankheads following him. Bloody tweakers. Following him so their mates could come inside his house while he was gone, leaving greasy, oily splotches on the floor and a streak running down the cabinets that took the finish off, bloody poofters pouring the same fluid on his silverware so it tarnished, then dumping the lot in the sink. Tweakers and witches in the caravan next door.

You've poison hemlock growing from under your fence, he said one morning to the red-haired woman who lived in the place, hoping to start conversation enough to detect her mob's purpose in harassing him.

Yeah, she said, I cast spells with it.

Later that same day, Martin came home from Grinch's to find a huge rodent lying in front of his shed door. Gypsy Feingold happened to notice—a rock chuck, he called it—because he himself had been going door-to-door asking after suspicious activity: his dogs had been weird, hacking wet globs from their lungs, acting listless. They refused to drink water from their usual bucket. Gypsy thought it was drug dealers. He said his wife Yara had a weed habit once and occasionally bought from the witch's trailer. Now and again dealers came around, from Spokane, he thought, trying to put a little pressure on her to start buying it again. He claimed regularly to see their trio of vehicles crossing the Camas Prairie.

This was about the time Martin started coming home from

his latest cabinet job to find minor chores undone—the bedding turned back, lid off the sugar bowl, newspaper spread on the table, food missing from the freezer. Plus, a notice had come in the post from an insurance broker about a claim against his beat-up Honda on a day when, as far as he knew, the auto had been parked. The key was broken off in the ignition and had to be turned with a pliers, a fact nobody knew save he himself. The night of the rock chuck he went scouting and noticed the back window of the car had been jigged open and left down.

The bloody bastards started in on his tools next. Down in a bucket of wrenches and screwdrivers he found a wad of lolly wrappers and buttons. Actual clothes buttons. Sent him into a rampage, searching the lot of his tools, of which he had accumulated a sizeable number, looking for more buttons and wrappers. He found a set of sockets that weren't his, full of dirt and grease like they'd been tossed about for a few dozen years, weird ID numbers etched into the handles. He called the coppers—the local and Idaho State Patrol—who never came to check it.

Then more disturbances in the house. Silverware disappearing from the old-fashioned tulip-flower set purchased at Gypsy and Yara Feingold's rummage sale with the words Rogers Silverplate clearly imprinted on the backs of the handles. Butter knives broken at the handle or one honed at the tip showing up in place of them, with a similar but not identical pattern and no imprint. *That's not a knoife! This is a knoife!*

Finally, people started following him, kids in beat-up autos with handheld two-ways, talking at night, even when he went out of his way around Winchester Lake or up to the Nez Perce tribe's patch of ground behind the lake where it was rumored they wanted to house a pack of wolves, for the sake of improving the spirit of the place, some claimed, but others claimed it was just the beginning of the Tribe's push to restock wolves throughout the countryside for the sake of killing off all the livestock and running off the whites for good. Arguments at

Buttress Hardware and Grinch's and the Old-Time's went on and on about the effect it would have on cattle ranching and elk and deer herds.

Story short and sweet, even rarely as he had to drive, every time he went to Lewiston for petrol or food, cars followed him down the windy Winchester grade and, upon his return, awaited him tucked into a gravel drive at the crest of the hill. He was certain he was not imagining it, so decided to report it to the FBI after an older green Buick with a single man alone followed him all the way to Lewiston, then drove hanging back as he made his way through downtown.

The federal building was large and stone with white columns, exterior walls made from stacks of rose-colored sandstone, the bronze statue of an Indian on a horse out front. According to the engraved label of the front artifice, it was formerly the Lewiston City Library. A man behind a desk in a white shirt and black tie listened to his speech, said it sounded worthy of opening a file, wrote a few details, asked for Martin's full name, address, and date of birth, green card, which coincidentally had arrived just days before, meaning he was finally eligible to start work on citizenship. Martin was worried about this last part. Green cards were worth a great amount of cash. Were they onto him? Were they after it? The agent suggested Martin pick up a camera and take pictures of the people following him. The bloke gave Martin his business card: Agent Luke Dijkstra, it said. Martin laughed. I am reporting missing tulip forks to a Netherlander.

I never would have thought of it that way, Agent Dijkstra said, not smiling.

Martin picked up a Kodak at a pawn shop for fairly cheap and a supply of film. Old, but it worked. The dunnyheads started pulling hats down to cover their faces when he drove by snapping photographs. He began to suspect the young punks were undercover bobbies, somehow tuned to the fact that John Glenn had a client who had enough of a supply to pay for chiropractic in illegal drugs. It was the only explanation. Why else would the city copper and the State Patrol not be interested in taking his report? He'd identified plates on eight vehicles—three finny older sedans big as Mellon's black one had been, and five big-powered utes. On the day he was to report back to Agent Dijkstra to hand over the camera film, four of the utes were in the parking lot at the Lewiston City Hall. He added this detail to his written report, in addition to a list of dates on which his vehicle had been tampered with, defining to the least detail the side effects of it, in particular the wheels wobbling on the axles like spinning plates. He wrote how he took the assembly apart, found a quarter-inch of slop and bark shreds from a stick put behind the rotors to hold the wheel in place. It would have lasted just long enough to get a good speed up on Hwy. 95, at which point the stick would've snapped. Wheel bearings, he had said to Agent Dijkstra, are held in place with a cotter pin. They don't come out unless pulled out.

The final blow came when Martin began finding what looked like specks of paint or caulking on his good clothes and weirdo rust-like stains on his bedding. Changing his sheets one day, he found an oblong imprint in his mattress, like somebody had set a bloody hot anvil on his bed. He had flipped the mattress over and a week later flipped it back, yet the imprint remained. He went for John Glenn's Baggie of white. Then he went about setting his first fire. A bonfire to burn the mattress and the bedding.

At night he and John talked about it. If a bloke wanted to frame you with a heinous crime, all he had to do is plant a few hairs in a mattress or a couch. If it was part of a cult that killed people, they needed scapegoats, but if was drug dealers, all somebody had to do was say they bought from you. Who could argue otherwise, John said. My word against your word. They can lock you away, even with no evidence.

Martin got to the point where he'd had enough and began making plans to move to Lewiston. He wanted a fresh start, but Gypsy Feingold wouldn't hear of him abandoning his belongings to be carted off, so Martin made a plan to build an even larger bonfire. Bugger the bastards if they thought they were going to get the better of *him*. John helped him hoist into a cone lengths of tamarack over the stack of possessions, the spire of the flame reaching higher than either man was tall, consuming clothing, upholstered cushions, books, stacks of newspapers. All except the tools, which Martin drove into the mountains on gravel roads, tossing one by one out of his decrepit Honda's window. He would not leave one shred to be used as evidence against him.

When events like this occur, John said, you either get paranoid or you turn spiritual.

Bloody hell, Martin said. All I can attest to is that I'm not going to end up buggered in a lockup because I tried an experiment one night. Even if I did like it. Even if I did keep the Baggie. Bollocks.

Martin considered whether to talk to Agent Dijkstra about purchasing a sidearm, but as a foreigner, he knew his limits. Nor was he sure he could ever pull the trigger on a human. He went instead to *The Lewiston Morning Tribune*, talked to a young, brown-haired bloke with a cigarette behind his ear, who was, of course, animated and curious about Martin's Aussie background, jotted notes onto a narrow notebook about the number of times Martin had gotten into his car to find the petrol gauge near empty, once even drained completely, unable to start, even though he never headed back to Winchester from Lewiston without filling the tank. Had Martin kept his gas receipts and odometer readings? He had. He had photographs: the gas cap on his bed's headrail; another time the gas cap door open; another time the driver's window was off its track, the gas cap on the seat.

The chap seemed doubly interested when Martin told him

how when he first got the little Honda there was a magnet box under the chassis with an extra ignition key, but when Martin went to retrieve it after he broke off the other key, it wasn't the same box but a larger, plastic one with an old wrench head and a white paper fob written in old man's scrawl that read, John Deere backhoe.

What do you do with backhoes? Martin asked the reporter. You dig bloody deep holes.

Which is the instant the reporter laid down his pencil and leaned back in his swivel chair.

When Martin's story reached the point of explaining the local law's ambivalence and the sawmill phone next to Morning Glory Acres ringing every time he left the house, the newsman's face shifted, the change in him speaking loud and grinding as a rasp: *mental case.*

In the days that followed, John Glenn packed his Trooper and left Winchester, saying he thought he'd try Missoula. It was the weird stuff in the pasture that finally did it for him, he said, and he feared for his and Martin's safety. Pieces of rusty, barbed wire and orange baling twine began appearing tied around fence posts, a day or two or three later switched off to another post, like a signal. John brought over a .22 rifle, taught Martin to aim and fire, using chipmunks as targets. As he was saying good-bye, John described to Martin how he opened a dresser drawer in his own apartment to find a few dozen empty .22 shells mixed in with a handful of dog food. He tried himself to see the Idaho County sheriff but was—he said he could feel it—immediately put on the wacko list.

Can't see the sheriff because he's not available the dispatcher says to me, John said. I'm a taxpayer, I say to her. I have rights to an appointment with the sheriff. *I'm happy to take your report,* the dispatcher says. Turns around and walks away. I try to tell her this is a time bomb up here. People are doing insane things. Crazy-making things. But she just walks away. He showed Martin the strange symbols drawn on the sidewalk next to his

Trooper. It was a symbol Martin had seen on cars around Winchester—paw prints, wolf's head silhouette. For certain some kind of gang, John said.

I don't know, Martin, my man, he continued. I did just today hear years back there was a string of bull mutilations over the hill in Culdesac, and the school mascot is the wolf. Made good money here, but clearly something isn't right. John Glenn handed out his ute's window the other two Baggies—the green one and the gray-brown. Here, he said. Keep it or throw it away. But don't go getting hooked, now. A little will enlighten you, but a lot will make you stupid. Another weird thing I just heard. Can't figure why it bothers me but it does. But did you know there never used to be trees on this place? Or on any of the Camas Prairie? The old Nez Perce kept it burned off for grazing ponies. Makes them sad to see trees here. Reminds them of the way things no longer are.

***

The sheila was a beaut. Legs to bloody American blonde hell and back. Her smell partway between ginger and gum tree and pepper. He found her tucked into the leather of one of Smitty's barrel-backed stools, but once the sex was over, as usual, he began calculating how to make his escape. What would the poor sheila think if she knew, curled into the cup of his shoulder and chest as if it were love, her hand browsing the dampness below his navel?

Directly on cue, she said it, similar version to all the others: You're the damned cutest thing, and I'm a fool for love. I'm almost thirty, want somebody regular and to get on with life. Might be hormones, I don't know, but were you ever crazy enough to pick up a girl at a bar, take her home and love her, next day drive to where they do things quick and cheap and marry her? That's all I'd require right now, a thirty-minute engagement. Thirty minutes is plenty of time to make up your mind about a girl.

That's only in storybooks, luv, he said, only on the telly.

You have the damned cutest accent, he kept expecting her to say.

Instead, climbing atop him yet again, she said, But they make those movies for a reason. Everybody wants to be loved at first sight, she said, tucking her feet beneath her pelvis, one apiece against either of his flanks.

Several hours later Martin was up to his elbows in dishwater. It was noon and the sheila had nicked off. Tammy. Nothing but the toast crumbs to show for it. Plus a line of tinnies. Never got his name right, not once. Called him Party Boy all night. Announced it to the room: *Marty the party boy's from Australia! He's seen kangaroos!*

The water sucked at him, siphoning him into another time and place, backward to a morning still in Perth, still married to Jenny Kay when he had his first event, standing under the shower head, the wall echoing the throb of rising mercury, silver and gelatinous, cold tile against his feet; Perth's hottest hits station pulsing with American tunes to the tempo of the water; the dial on the waterproof radio swimming before his eyes as he dropped into the mercury and the smell of soap, of water heated, the floating away of his natural oils, his skin's surface tension broken. He once worked in-hospital. He'd favored talking to the chemists. He knew the ways of soap — soap in dishwater breaks up grease. *Breaks the particle bonds.* At least standing there in his apartment in Lewiston, Idaho, he did not seize. At least that much had changed. At least he did not lose consciousness.

America taught him to drink coffee. A good stop in Lewiston was Java the Hut. A local shop, and he preferred local shops over chains. A girl was seated in his usual seat that morning who called herself Maya. Blonde, again, but older, not as raspy as the sheila Tammy the night before. Martin reckoned Maya was feeling crook, the way she leaned her head and got quiet.

Said she'd contracted a muscle weakness which initially qualified her for the dole until some government agent claimed it
was a mental issue, not physical, therefore not a disability, left
her to fend for herself.

Right off the bat, then, a subject they had in common.
Bloody white-shirt bureaucratic drongos. Couldn't calculate
what brought on his seizures, either, so his file read *Schizoaffec-
tive Disorder/Bipolar Type*, which made people labor over him
in a particularly puzzled way. Bloody transplanted American
Pommies choking their pens to come up with ways to dispatch
people. Was taking a blue moon to get himself naturalized because of that diagnosis, all that studying, which he was doing in part to try to qualify for the special disability dole for
foreigners who have worked under a green card. He needed
ten years of paying into the system, rather than doing the spo-
radic work he'd been doing for cash. Green card or no, that's
how people dealt with him so far. Pay under the table so they
didn't have to trudge through the paperwork. No matter. Some
chook-brained Idaho medico decided he didn't have seizures,
rather a mental disorder, so no disability dole for him on the
horizon.

People talked to Martin, for some reason, about their sick-
nesses. Opened up and started a conversation. Made him talk
back about his own troubles. He didn't mention *it*, however—
his *it*—except to sheilas. Women understood where blokes
didn't. Women understood why a man might walk around
with a memento in his rucksack for a span of years. Men listened for a tick or two, then their eyes glazed, then back to
ballplayers and politicos. Women moaned in a small, sad way,
reached a hand to his arm. Martin always asked first, but not
if and until it seemed right to the flow of conversation: *mind if
I show you something?* The younger ones got defensive and gig-
gly, expecting perversion. The wiser ones raised an eyebrow,
sat, waited.

This one, Maya, didn't arch her brow but said, Only if it

isn't alive or illegal.

No worries, he said, her letting him eye her, letting him size her up while she sipped a mug of coffee. He let time stand for a beat, then Martin passed Maya the Ziplock with the tiny muslin-colored hospital cap inside, knit like a thin cotton sock, and the two Polaroids. In one he was holding a baby obviously alive. In the other, the baby looked dead.

They talked through the day and until the Java manager politely told them he was closing. It was long after dark. Nine p.m. They'd been talking since two in the afternoon. Maya, who in one day made him for the first time since Jenny Kay feel the imprint of the word *marriage*. He liked the jovial nature of their conversation, the sparkling words. He talked. She listened. She talked. He listened. Subjects came easily, the downs and lows of these past years for both of them. He told her he wanted to wean off medication in exchange for exercise, Taoism, and meditation. How embarrassed and unfair the arrest was that landed him in jail overnight, strictly because he was a long-hair. He wanted to take classes, albeit he had no delusions about a degree. He'd dog-paddle 'til he wore out, but he planned to give it a good go. Meantime he'd continue his conferences with Val at ILC, sitting in her office chair staring at her nameplate until he got his rights to his own finances back, then kiss the mothers good-bye. Of course he didn't tell Maya that the reason for the tight control at this point was that he'd balled Val Corsica once, in her office. She'd broken a big rule. Martin could get her in all brands of trouble. Her way of handling it was to demonize him, tighten the official choke chain, make it tough on him as she possibly could.

He relayed events on the levy that led to his arrest to Maya. He carried guilt about it, but he didn't know why. Neither did his shrink. *Ask Jesus! Ask Jesus!* a bloke had run up saying. He knew what he'd ask Jesus, he said to the man, what the bloody hell you doing trying to impersonate me? Martin then lifted a beer from the Esky to hand to the chap to shut him up. *The*

Igloo. Only in America would they take a bloody thing you put ice *into* and call it the same as an item made *out* of it. That was the moment the coppers showed up. The moment he handed a beer to the Jesus bloke.

Stand right there and show your ID. Move slow. Keep your hands where I can see them, the first one said. Martin turned from where he was seated to face the wheel of a bike, the shiny spokes, dark then light, dark then light, reflecting the levy's path lights.

You from this country, sir? the officer had said. If you are, then you know when an officer asks for your ID, you show him your ID. Another officer on a bike pulled up. Both in black shorts, black shirts, black everything. Their helmets looked like ant heads, marked in gold letters on the front with LPD.

This is 691, the first officer said into the air.

Go ahead, the little square radio on his shoulder said.

I'll be 10-97 on the Lewiston Levy at milepost 3. Single white male. Possible 922. Standing by for wants and warrants.

You know it's illegal to drink on the levy, sir? Would you mind standing up, sir? the first officer said. What's your name and date of birth?

Martin looked around himself. Three questions. Three at once. He'd lost that hole in the ground. If he had it, he'd climb down it. Wouldn't they look funny, watching him climb down the ladder, watching him heading down to the rabbit to drink tea? *Watership Down!* he'd say, because that's what he'd think. *Watership Down!*

Sir? Sir, the officer said, would you stand up now?

The second officer held back, thumbs in his holster belt. Martin liked him better, so he leaned forward to crane his neck and squint for a look closer. Hey! Hey! he said, pointing toward the second officer. She's a sheila! Bloody hell!

The second officer looked down toward the ground.

Sir, the first officer said, once more: please stand.

All right, all right, all right. Bloody hell. Bloody dipsticks,

Martin said, pushing himself butt up in the air until his arm and hands made a triangle with his feet. When he got stuck there, the second officer put an arm under his armpit to help him the rest of the way up. Crikey. I'm bloody Croak-o-dial Dun-day. That ain't no movie, mate. The real deal. Got me a wife and everything. Well, I did. But bloody, hell, mate. Don't twist me like that.

Martin felt the night blacken to swamp around him. He watched midnight blue suck and swallow both officers' faces. He thought there ought to be a sweet gum tree growing right out of this pavement and this great river. Who would call it a Snake River? He hadn't seen any snakes. Jesus fucking hell. Crikey hell. They ought to be a gillagong tree.

Martin started to laugh. A gillagong tree, he said to the officers. There ain't no gillagong tree. Gillagong's a town. Said it wrong 'sall, Mate. There ain't no gillagong tree. 'Sa town, mate. Martin felt himself weaving, but the second officer held him by the armpits so he just let it be. Then the first officer talked into his shoulder and a third officer drove up and all three walked Martin down the hill to the prowler with its flinching, warbling lights.

Be advised, 619, this is a 5150. Case manager en route, the shoulder said.

Dispatch, this is 701, copy that, the second officer said.

My Igloo! Martin said, as the first officer instructed him to lower his head so he wouldn't bump it on the hood of the patrol car. My Igloo!

Wrenching loose and running back for it earned him the charges of resisting and elude.

***

The second time around in Winchester, a decade after he arrived the first time, the atmosphere had definitely changed. It had become a tourist town, with a big log lodge and trinket shops, a grocer's, more cafes, a place for lattes and muffins. He went straightaway and took a job washing dishes at the Old-Time, got hired to tend the tavern a few nights a week at Grinch's. Bought himself a small set of tools and worked up sets of rosette drawer pulls to sell at Buttress Hardware the rest of the time.

Six months now and life was peaceful without the bloody Haldol. He thought he should get a telephone, but then he'd be tempted to call Val. Or Maya. And he really didn't want to call either one. He was plenty entertained in the sheila category by talking to Annalesa with a calling card at the pay phone outside the washeteria. Plus, occasionally, to Arlette, who had started to gray at about the same rate that he had, over his morning eggs and bacon at the Old-Time.

MELINDA PANEPINTO

SHE HATED THINKING about her ex, Nathan. Good-looking as sin, but needy. Wanted a mother, not a wife. There wasn't much to do once you graduated high school in Sturgis, South Dakota, but wait tables until time for the motorcycle rally that had in recent years started up and looked to keep repeating annually for the money it brought to town, then dream to hook up and ride west with a good-looking biker. At least that had been Melinda's lead-in for the story she told about herself.

The rest of it featured being born on the Pine Ridge reservation to a mixed-blood nurse and a government contractor who built houses for a new agency called Housing and Urban Development. Her mother worked at the Indian Health Service hospital, nursing people back from gunshot wounds and the impacts of alcoholism. Melinda's largest memory featured walking into the kitchen when she was seven or so to find her mother, still in her starched white uniform from the night shift, head down at the kitchen table with the local newspaper in her lap and her father staying home from work that day. Her parents hid the newspaper, but Melinda got up in the middle of the night with a flashlight to look for it although she immediately wished she hadn't because of the feeling she felt in her stomach, which never in all these years totally went away.

A baby was dead. An Indian baby. A relative of her mother's. A car backed out of a carport at a house her father had built and ran over its head. *Dead on arrival*, the title said. Her mother must have seen what that baby looked like with its head smashed in. Melinda kept herself occupied for days and days, drawing pictures of a baby's head with a tire track on it. After a while her mother came out of the bedroom with her nurse uniform on and went back to work, thanking Melinda at some point for being so well-behaved while she was not feeling well. Soon after they started driving Melinda to Sturgis in the big International for school, returning on Fridays to bring her home for the weekend. After a few months of that, her mother got a job at the hospital in Sturgis, and the entire family moved, leaving her father to make the commute.

Flashy-eyed. That's how she described Nathan when she first met him. He was off for the summer, looking for jobs, in the middle of his PhD courses at the University of Wisconsin. He came into her diner loaded for bear—black leather chaps and matching jacket. She might have been only eighteen, but she couldn't help looking at the denim-covered rounds, front and back, where the chaps came together just below the belt buckle but didn't take up again until they hit the thighs. This manner of dress had trained her to look at that part of a man's body before she looked at his eyes. Lots of men—dozens and dozens of them, came to the diner dressed like that during the motorcycle rally, and her line of sight automatically zeroed in on the region where the leather was not—that round, blue, denim-colored space. But she noticed Nathan's bright eyes first, that's how sparkly and full of life they were.

Melinda loved educated types. Her mother and father brought her up to believe the pursuit of an education worth whatever time, effort, and money it required. Even if it didn't enhance your salary, it enhanced daily living. You learned to make informed decisions. You only had to look at shifting clusters of Sioux boys and long-braided girls pregnant as soon as they commenced menses to see the difference between earning a high school diploma and not. Call it white brainwashing, which is just what it was. But if you've got to fit in to thrive, then make yourself fit.

The youngest first-time mother she ever heard of was nine. The boy, seventeen, was beaten to a bloody lump by the girl's father, a white. The FBI was called in, the boy was charged as an adult, and the crimes looked on as felonies, so both the boy and the girl's father got locked away for a good while. Melinda never heard what happened to the girl.

Those were magical days, meeting Nathan and letting herself come under his spell. Melinda lost her virginity to him gladly, even if she had no idea what it was about her that he loved, but he returned summer after summer until he finished his degree, then asked if she'd come back to Wisconsin with him, become the wife of a college professor. That fate suited her mother and father just fine.

Spend your time in the library, her father advised. Join film groups. Take a class.

Which is exactly what Melinda did that first winter and the winter after. Then the first pair of babies arrived, providing her with an earthy education and a role she embraced with vigor. Madison, Wisconsin, had a population of exceptional midwives. Melinda gave birth to the twins, Angie and Terrell, seated crouched with legs spread and Nathan embracing her from behind, supporting and protecting her. The vibration of love in the atmosphere of that cedar-lined room was thick as Wisconsin cheese and overwhelming enough to cause each of them—Nathan, Melinda, the midwife, the doula—to shout with evangelical joy when each baby burst forth.

Angie and Terrell arrived screaming too hard to make a sound until they caught breath, then the wail was enough to bruise an eardrum. The midwife talked about it as the single most ecstatic moment in her career. The revelation was one of pure joy. The doula, who had coached thousands of births, and the midwife, who was nearing oversight of her three-hundredth birth, said she'd never witnessed anything of such cosmic proportions as the entry of Angie and Terrell into the world. Ezekiel was born two years later, followed in nine months by twins Benjamin and Marshall, all born the same place with the same cast and the same set of circumstances, but none was so riveting and mystifying as that first little boy and girl.

As happens, the marriage died. Neither of them knew how

or when. Melinda thought it had to do with Nathan giving up on his love of motorcycle racing. They were otherwise going about living a merged existence, raising kids, Nathan lecturing and teaching the occasional community workshop for extra money. He published books and wrote papers—an average university professor trying to keep a niche carved for himself. He regularly admitted he'd been at the right place at the right time to get his job. PhDs were not so common in the fifties. All a man needed was a degree in hand to get a position. Now they wanted to open up education to even the poor with more scholarships. There were rumors of even the government stepping in to provide funding by the early sixties. As he told Melinda, once college enrollments started going up, the ranks of specialized professors would go down, giving the mess over to a population of teachers who had no time for research. Melinda listened to this kind of talk gladly, diaper pins in mouth, searching for car keys, pot roast in oven, bourbon and seltzer in hand, holding wheel-armed teenagers back from each other. Then one day Nathan came home with his briefcase and boxes of books and office supplies and said, I've been offered a job. Columbia. Please forgive me, Melinda. I don't want to take you or the kids. They're grown. It's time for you to build a life. I just want to be off by myself.

Oh, *of course*, there was another, younger woman, but Melinda wasn't thinking about her. She was thinking about time, of all the years, and whether wasted or whether the new ones were being better spent. She alternately fumbled with and hacked at the noose that was her divorce. Eventually she made her way to Missoula and tried to move on by helping others through various alternative holistic therapies and Tarot and birth chart readings. Skills she developed through correspondence courses. Weekends were hardest, often spent sitting with a sketch pad, drawing new renditions of an old image— fields and fields of dead children, smashed and flattened about the head and middle, dark, malicious tire treads running from head to toe and side to side, a huge monster truck idling in the background, gearing up for another go-around.

***

Using holistic treatments on a court-ordered patient wasn't entirely inappropriate, but it probably wasn't good business. Martin Tuor was a political firecracker, as far as politics extended to mental health in Idaho and the Independent Living Center. State agencies were trying to make a success case of him because he was Aussie and good-looking and everybody loved him. She and her boss Val were both guilty of sexually harassing the man. Once in a while she suspected things might have gone further than that with Val and Martin.

Always fishing for a miracle cure for his problems, he carried around a backpack with enough health food supplements to fill a picnic basket. He chatted about crystals and seers and astrology. World religion. Every new doctrine was a miracle cure. He did weight lifting, yoga, meditation—and reported on his experiences with all. Then he began traveling to holistic fairs, often generating enthusiasm in a group of ILC clients and taking a collection to fill somebody's gas tank, which then for weeks had participating clientele chattering about how they'd benefited from Reiki, Shen, flower essences, aromatherapy, acupuncture. Not that all that many ILC clients had cars, but Martin's girlfriend Maya had one, and she always seemed to be game for travel.

Her State of Idaho superiors refused to allow her to pay for the trips with ILC money (one legislator called it snake oil to her face), no matter how hard she argued for the therapeutic relevance of travel, activity, and focus. She kept a quote Martin himself made one day when they were brainstorming ways to raise money to help people get out into the world to see and do things. Most of these people aren't sick, he'd said. They're just bored.

They first talked about amplification when Martin came to Melinda's house for dinner. Martin struggled almost daily with his addictions. Liquor and pot did not go with Dilantin or Haldol. He shouldn't drink coffee or smoke cigarettes, but he did. His mind was an antenna, tuning into every sight and sound at random speeds. She'd invited him several times, but he'd been hesitant, said he was living with Maya, clearly putting a sexual spin on Melinda's invitation. One she had to make clear was appreciated but not the best call.

As luck went, and as had rarely happened in her history of conducting these sessions, the client had no iconoclastic movements. They set the subject aside, but later, Melinda realized a truth—she'd never treated a male. Her treatment studio in downtown Missoula, from which she earned her living for many years, was open to both genders. Men had walked through the door, but not one had laid dollars on the counter.

A catalyst to almost any process is plain time, which Melinda had plenty of, so she started taking Marty home on Friday nights, cooking dinner with him, going for walks, plugging in a movie. It took three months—*three months*—of linguine and other forms of pasta, pulled pork, enchiladas, frittatas, burgers, and macaroni salad, but one night on the back deck over glasses of cherry smoothies, Melinda finally saw the brief flutter of Marty's fingers against his sternum. Over and over but just barely, talking about his childhood in Jelico and the caravan park, fantasizing what might have been had he and his wife, the mother of his baby, met sooner or figured how to stay together longer. The fingers fluttered again and again, a pale but regular rhythm. Melinda watched it and counted. Eight, ten, a dozen drumbeats. The right hand, ring finger, middle, then pointer, then all three landing briefly together. *Triddle-um. Triddle-um.*

Finally, on the twelfth Friday night, after lingcod in parchment and mahogany rice, sitting on the deck with homemade apricot-blueberry sorbet, Martin fantasized about where he'd go if he left Lewiston. Geographic solutions went with depression. She was no PhD, but she knew depression couldn't be solved with a pill. Or hooch, or sex, or a change of place, or any of the remedies people sought. Melinda believed a person could trace depression back to one single pinpoint in their life. The moment life first bites you—the moment it makes it clear you have no control, nothing is certain, and, therefore, nothing one-hundred percent matters. Lucky people glimpsed it and recovered and moved forward freed by the knowledge. Many spent their lives using all means to try to forget it: work, drugs, sex, booze. Some, like Martin, couldn't deal with it and sucked it into their bodies. Worst were those who'd rather die than live with it. Martin wasn't suicidal, but it made everyone sad that he couldn't stay on his own feet for long.

She'd come to think of it as *the interruption*. She thought that up until then we still have our spiritual umbilical cord direct to the inner web that joins us all. That moment we are injured is the moment the cord is severed. Never spank a baby, Melinda used to tell couples in her childbirth classes. Being disrupted as a baby is spiritual hell. It takes a shaman to pull you out of it.

So, it had taken twelve weeks, twelve Friday night dinners, and twelve discussions of the Missoula flood's geology and eastern Washington scablands and Hells Canyon, Martin's favorite topics. But as soon as Melinda said, Flutter your chest, followed by his blank look and then the command again, *Flutter your chest.* Martin choked on his smoothie and began to cry. Uncontrollable. For so many minutes on end that Melinda thought she might have to do CPR. He was crying so hard he wasn't breathing.

Finally, after perhaps thirty minutes of convulsive sobbing, he sputtered it out with enough saliva and nasal snot to fill a handkerchief: *the nail, he stepped on a fencing nail, and what was it doing in the house and why didn't he pull it out as soon as he saw it or tell somebody and the way the doctor's office smelled sour-*

sweet from ether and the way he wished a nail had stabbed him in the heart after his mother screamed and screamed cuffing him and boxing his ears while Pops tried and tried to shush her and calm her down over his clumsiness costing every dime the family had then the cross his playmates built and the visiting American woman who nicked off with the hired hand and his own mother who first fell crook in the head and then one day walked down the Drury Road by herself never to be heard from again all those years of drowning in mercury when it wasn't mercury at all but barrels and barrels and barrels and barrels of the melted molten zinc of carpentry nails.

PART V

STEPHANIE CLARK-DRUKER

WADE NELSON CLARK-DRUKER plied his way into the world on February 2, at 4:06 p.m., at St. Luke's in Boise. Although at first outspoken against the idea of her mother having a baby at fifty, by six weeks in, grown sister Becky was proving to be devoted to her role as older sister—and an enormous help.

You're old, she had said, all those months back, stirring honey into tea, dark bangs cut at an angle from brow to temple, partially but purposefully obscuring her lazy eye. I'm the one who should be having babies, not a potential grandmother. What about Downs? What if it's born deformed?

Who says you can't love a baby with deformities? We're pregnant and we're having a child. You're going to have to get your mind around it. Neither mentioning the droop to Becky's right eye, the patch she'd had to wear in elementary school.

Yet once Wade was born, Becky rode her bicycle over daily to pitch in. She insisted on sanitizing bottles for freezing Stephanie's surplus breast milk even though the latest research said it wasn't necessary.

It was not exactly warm, but there was elation enough in the air to imagine spring. Stephanie watched quick-moving cloud clusters and desert-hued shades of amber and coral spread skyward from the eastern horizon to envelope Boise. A *National Geographic* moment. She turned to check on Wade, who was fed and back to sleeping, tucked into his bassinet. From inside the house, the sound of Glenn's vague snore.

It was her maternal hormones, she supposed, inspiring emotions, memories, and spur-of-the-moment tears. Flickers of scenes from Wade's birth. The beauty of the sunrise. Then for no reason, the image of Becky's biological father. Another pregnancy. Another birth. Another era in the culture of her life.

She never allowed herself to think about him, not even in the wake of Becky's many and myriad questions over the years. All Stephanie ever let on was that in her search for herself, she took a cross-country bike trip. It was after the age of free love but before herpes and AIDS. A fellow traveler. From Australia. Not once in her life had she ever used birth control. She and Glenn had long thought themselves barren—although inexplicably so, since various medical assessments over the years had declared otherwise—only to conceive after two decades of marriage. Not even Becky with her biological father's naïve rationalism had been able to dissuade them: they *were* taking the risk; they *were* having a late-life baby.

The stack of books representing next semester's load of his astronomy and her geography courses sat on the desk near Glenn's recliner. She'd put them there to remind them both there was still a world outside their family's new daily life. Diapers and immunization schedules aside, eventually sabbatical would end, and they'd have to get back to earning a living. They had piles of lists documenting late-night talks and ideas. Their combined portfolios from the university were substantial. A small house in a cheaper town subsidized by whatever else they could bring in as adjuncts or high school substitutes might stretch it long enough and far enough to get Wade at least through high school, if not college. Lean living did not frighten either of them, and Becky was self-sufficient and busy with her own life—if not quite yet focused enough to choose a career. They hoped rural living would foster in Wade a quieter spirit than Becky's. Stephanie was willing to give up just about anything to gamble on the possibility of that happening.

From out there, the doorbell was hard to distinguish from a bird call, as kitschy as that was, so she couldn't be certain that's what she heard, but then for sure came the noise of water from a toilet's flushing echoed down the hallway through the French doors between the deck and dining room, as if funneling down a hollow cone. That Argentinian slate they loved so much on their next-door neighbor Angelina's hearth had turned out to be unforgiving to bare feet, even as warm as Boise's summers could get. It never seemed to lose its chill. They both were concerned about cold floors with a crawling baby.

Stephanie? Glenn's voice sifted through space, made her want him. Wonderful thing, being married to someone whose voice you love hearing. Doorbell woke me up. You know a Dale McMurtrey? You just got a special-delivery letter.

No, but I'll be right there, she called, pausing to appreciate the half disc of sun pushing above the horizon, its yellow force slightly fuzzed by woodstove smoke, the season in transition. A poetic morning. She'd suggest they make sandwiches, pack a cooler, pick up Becky, and head to the mountains. Give Wade his first experience in nature, a look at the world he'd been born to.

ACKNOWLEDGMENTS

While I wrote this as fiction, working primarily from imagination, the idea for this story first flickered when I met the real Martin Tuor, formerly of Sydney, who took the last open seat on a Greyhound Bus I was riding in August of 2001. The events of September 11, 2001, later rendered him technically trapped in our country. I've always been struck by the fact that I was on that bus on a whim, recording people and circumstances that eventually became part of my novel *Dove Creek*. Not once during our eight-hour conversation during the journey from Chicago to Minneapolis did I consider that I was entering the world of another tale—one that would require five years of research and almost as many of writing.

Primarily, however, the story owes its telling to Dennis Bortz, of Lewiston, Idaho, who shared his difficult life history over a number of interview sessions. Information about life as a mental health client in Idaho otherwise came from the testimony of people who've been shuffled through the system and who preferred to remain anonymous. In some cases, their stories are merged with knowledge I gained while working as a student nurse at an out-patient mental health clinic in Pendleton, Oregon.

Others who lent significant support in the writing of this book include artist Jenny Kay Snyder, Rich Wandschneider, Ric Bombaci, Janis Carper, and the Fishtrap Writer-in-Residence Program, The Imnaha Writer's Retreat and the Driver family, Scott McMurtrey, Alan McMurtrey, Jeanne Sumner, Melinda Artz, Lisa Panepinto, Lance and Andi Olsen, Kathleen and Amandus Wolff, Carol Sano, Janie Tippetts, Tom Hampson, Sheryle and Chuck Roberts, Sallee and Dave Tanzey and the Imnaha Store and Tavern, survivors of the Imnaha River flood of '96, *The Wallowa County Chieftain*, my sons Gabe and

David, their families, and now and forever, my beloved Phil.

Thank you to Andrea Mason, who read and commented on an early draft.

Special thank you to my dear father, Albert Coomer, whose lovable idiosyncrasies are reflected in the character Edmonds Tuor.

Also, thanks to Jim and Ruth May at Reflections Inn for the solitude and splendid creative space.

Lastly, to Fawkes Press and Jodi Thompson for reigniting the dream, and my great creative team. Galaxies of thanks and appreciation to my unflinching editor Nancy Casey, who endured more backtalk from me than she should have, as well as Vicki Sly of Broome, who made certain I rendered the English language and the country of Australia correctly.

The following volumes were either a great influence on the imagining of *Jagged Edge of the Sky* or were consumed or consulted as I was writing:

All but the Waltz by Mary Clearman Blew
American Dreams: Lost & Found by Studs Terkel
Australia edited by Hartley Grattan
Australia 2001 by Gareth Powell
Breaking Clean by Judy Blunt
Cultures of the World: Australia by Vijeya and Sundran Rajendra
Burning Fence: A Western Memoir of Fatherhood by Craig Lesley
Cold Beer and Crocodiles, A Bicycling Journey into Australia by Roff Smith
Down Under by Bill Bryson
Eyewitness Travel Guides: Sydney by Ken Brass and Kirsty McKenzie
Famous Australian Art: S.T. Gill's Rural Australia, edited by Bob Raftopoulos
Gap Creek: The Story of a Marriage by Robert Morgan

Girl Imagined by Chance by Lance Olsen
Goddesses in Every Woman by Jean Shinoda Bolen, M.D.
How I Came West, and Why I Stayed by Alison Baker
In a Sunburned Country by Bill Bryson
It is No Secret: The Story of a Stolen Child by Donna Meaham
Kick the Tin by Doris Kartinyeri
Life is so Good by George Dawson and Richard Glaubman
Mutant Message Down Under by Marlo Morgan
My Place by Sally Morgan
Owning it All by William Kittredge
Shadow Child: A Memoir of the Stolen Generation by Rosalee Fraser
The Larousse Encyclopedia of Mythology, introduction by Robert Graves
The Fatal Shores: The Epic of Australia's Founding by Robert Hughes
The River Why by David James Duncan
The Road from Coorain by Jill Ker Conway
This House of Sky by Ivan Doig
Thornbirds by Colleen McCollough
Tonguing the Zeitgeist by Lance Olsen
True North by Jill Ker Conway
Women of the Bush: Forces of Desire in the Australian Cultural Tradition by Kay Schaffer

Spooky at first, but later laughable, over the nine years this book was being researched, written, and revised, each time Phil and I went to the movie rental store, the film we rented ended up being about Australians and/or set in Australia. At times we chose them on purpose, because I was obsessed with all things Aussie, but more often than not, the film's packaging would give no indication that the story was set down under. Although I failed to keep a list, Phil will testify to my having watched several hundred Australian films. It is fair to say my storytelling and language use are fully influenced by the rhythms of the spoken words of Aussie actors and actresses. Thanks to the age of the Internet, I was also able to view more than twelve hundred photographs of the Western Australia region, where *Jagged Edge of the Sky* is set. The novel's geographic names are fictional, and the villages are conglomerates of places I visited through the reading of various memoirs. In this way, they are based on wide spots in the road that do exist or did exist in the past. I owe Merl Chatcolet's fear of the people of Kuyunga to the film *Wolf Creek*.

SUPPORT FOR THE AUTHOR

News of books travel best by word of mouth. If you appreciated *Jagged Edge of the Sky*, do let the world know! Recommend to a friend, your local library or book club, or write a small review and post it with your favorite online retailer.

ABOUT THE AUTHOR

Paula Marie Coomer is a poet, novelist, essayist, cookbook author, and a writer of short fictions. The daughter of over two hundred years of Kentucky Appalachian farmers and storytellers, she lived most of her childhood in the industrial Ohio River town of New Albany, Indiana. Ms. Coomer's other books include *Dove Creek, Summer of Government Cheese, Blue Moon Vegan, Blue Moon Vegetarian*, and two collections of poetry. Coomer lives near the mouth of Hells Canyon in southeast Washington State, where she teaches writing and organizes writing retreats and workshops.

LEARN MORE

Discover more about Paula Marie Coomer and her books and work at www.paulamariecoomer.com. Sign up for her Rare and Occasional File to receive updates and free gifts! You can also reach her by email at coom1286@hotmail.com.

Connect with her on social media—
- ❖ On Twitter:
  @PMCoomer
- ❖ On Facebook:
  https://www.facebook.com/paula.coomer.3
  and
  https://www.facebook.com/paulamariecoomerauthor
- ❖ On Goodreads:
  https://www.goodreads.com/author/show/1018775.
  Paula_Marie_Coomer
- ❖ On Pinterest:
  https://www.pinterest.com/paulamcoomer/

Book Paula Marie Coomer for a reading, signing, book club talk, community presentation, or workshop, by going to http://www.paulamariecoomer.com/about-paula-marie-coomer/scheduling-information/

For press information go to
http://www.paulamariecoomer.com/press/press-kit/

OTHER BOOKS BY PAULA MARIE COOMER

Summer of Government Cheese
This collection of odd and sometimes disturbing short stories about the Pacific Northwest working class is not easy reading. Some stories experiment with form and language. People get raped. Women are murdered. Some people are gay. Some are liars. Some are old. Some are suffering betrayal at the hands of those they love. Some are migrant workers. Some are intellectually disabled. Some are suffering post-traumatic stress. Some are enslaved by American corporations. Readers who enjoy quirky characters and long, winding narratives, will appreciate these stories.

Dove Creek
This fictional memoir tells the story of Patricia Faye Morrison, whose life spans from the mountains of Kentucky to the mountains of Idaho and a nursing job on the Nez Perce Indian reservation. The story chronicles her quest for meaning and identity as she goes about her duties, learning about and recognizing her own heritage in Native American culture. Recovering from a difficult divorce, Patricia frets about raising her two sons and struggles with self-destruction. Her story is one of perseverance and survival as she winds her way through the "Lesson of the Seven Directions," a Nez Perce myth about finding one's way to a true and fulfilling life.

Nurses Who Love English
These poems chronicle the Sept. 11, 2001, attacks from the emergence of war to a life wobbling under the impact of world events: the loss of livelihood caused by federal budget cuts,

a year of unemployment, record gasoline prices, and mega-inflation. In the shadows, events that should have been celebrations become struggles: the empty nest, children marrying and becoming parents themselves, finding late-life love. Lyrical, emotional, and, in the words of poet Paisley Rekdal, "both tough-minded yet fragile," the poems in this collection reveal the conflicting perspectives of the rural American West during one of the most difficult times in modern history.

Blue Moon Vegetarian: Reflections, Recipes, and Advice for a Plant-Based Diet

Part memoir, part cookbook, this health-and-nutrition how-to chronicles Kentucky-born former nurse Paula Marie Coomer as she and her fiancé go vegetarian—and ultimately vegan—while also planning a mid-life wedding, adopting a shelter dog, and remodeling their two-story Victorian. Writing with honesty and humor, Coomer tells the story of two people alternately thriving and suffering as they adjust to a new way of eating, living, and loving. With advice from a former public health professional and over fifty original, plant-based recipes, this thought-provoking book is perfect for anyone concerned about their own health, the health of their loved ones, and the health of our planet.

Blue Moon Vegan

Paula Marie Coomer partners with baker Jan Calvert to raise the culinary bar with over one hundred original recipes, all of which are based on plant-derived ingredients and are also gluten-free. Ranging from luscious side dishes to scrumptious breads, snacks, pastries, and innovative main courses, these easy-to-follow recipes will inspire both new and experienced vegans as well as omnivores looking to add a few meatless meals to the menu. The book includes dozens of pages of nutrition and cooking information. Beautifully photographed and formatted for easy use, Blue Moon Vegan is destined to become a well-used favorite for cooks of all persuasions.

DISCUSSION QUESTIONS

Who and/or what is this book about? How do your ideas about this change throughout the novel?

There are a lot of people featured in this book. Do you like some of them more than others? Do you dislike some of them? Do you think the narrator likes/dislikes the various characters?

Draw a "family tree" that shows how the characters in the novel are related to one another. In addition to blood relationships, show other important bonds, such as strong friendships or shared experiences. At what point in your reading of the novel did you feel like you had a grasp of how all the characters are related?

The chapters in the book are not at all of equal length. Do you think that's a reflection on the importance of the character in the big story? Take Merl Chatcolet, for example. The chapter with his name is very short. What else do you know about Merl? Could you write his biography? What role does he play in his community? Are there other characters in other communities in the novel playing similar roles?

"Economy of language" is the phrase that describes the effort an author makes to write sentences and paragraphs where every word matters—no extras and no fluff. Identify some passages in the novel where the economy of language is particularly high. Look for places where a lot of detail (information, imagery) is conveyed in just a few lines, or even a few words.

What role does poverty play in the novel? How do you define "poverty"? Which characters do you think would have made different decisions if they'd had more resources? What resources? What decisions? Is the lack of resources always connected to poverty?

At the end of the book, the author lists works that were influential in the writing of Jagged Edge of the Sky. Are you familiar with some of them? What influence do you think they might have had? Some of the books on the list are stories of people whose lives are interconnected over generations. Do you think *Jagged Edge of the Sky* is a "typical" family saga? How is it like and not-like other novels of this kind that you have read?

What is alternative fiction? Alternative to what? What is the opposite of "alternative"? Consciously or unconsciously, readers bring expectations to a novel. What expectations of yours were thwarted? What "rules" of novel-writing did the author seem to be breaking? At some point, this rule-breaking can become too much for readers and they give up. Does this novel run that risk? Is the satisfaction of understanding how all the pieces are interrelated worth the effort it takes to remember it all and figure it out?

CPSIA information can be obtained
at www.ICGtesting.com
Printed in the USA
BVOW00s2317011216
469567BV00001B/11/P